The Lesotho Herders Video Project

Explorations in
Visual Anthropology

by
Chuck Scott

intervention press

In association with the Centre for Cultural and Media Studies,
University of Natal

Published by
Intervention Press
Castenschioldsvej 7
DK-8270 Højbjerg

Photographs by
C. Scott, T. Quinlan, and
S. Schmidt

Cover design by
Peter Ian Crawford and Chuck Scott

Typeset in Denmark by
Hanne Buhl, Gjern

Printed in Denmark by
AKA-Print, Århus

Published in association with the
Centre for Cultural and Media Studies,
University of Natal, Durban, South
Africa

ISBN 87-89825-04-7

Preface

This book is based on a 'long essay' written in November 1991 for an Honours degree at the Centre for Cultural and Media Studies (CCMS), University of Natal in Durban, South Africa. What started out as a course requirement evolved into a challenging and frustrating attempt to reconcile theory and practice which I have termed 'fitting fieldwork into theoretical frameworks'. Analyzing the three very demanding field trips described in this document led to an equally demanding exploration of a field that inherits a set of problems from two disciplines concerned with representation of the 'other'. This uneasy union of anthropology and film-making has generated complex debates of its own which grapple with questions crucial to both. I have attempted to map this theoretical terrain in the context of our own experience of the process of producing a 'community video' with a group of livestock herders in Lesotho.

Eighteen months after this report was initially written, a further field trip, and countless hours of sub-titling later, we have finally moved from 'process' to 'product' with the completion of a 40 minute video entitled *BALISANA - Herders of Lesotho*. However, the project has yet to reach closure as we still have to take this video back to Lesotho for screenings to the herders, village communities, local authorities and government officials.

I would like to express my thanks and appreciation to the following people: Anthropologist Tim Quinlan who made the project possible. Without his years of experience of working with the Basotho people and his knowledge of the country, customs and language, this project could never have happened; Co-producer Steve Schmidt, for his critical eye and keen wit; Professor Keyan Tomaselli of CCMS for encouraging me to look further and delve deeper; and Peter Ian Crawford for acknowledging our 'intervention'.

Chuck Scott
Durban, May 1993

Contents

Introduction

The ability of anthropologists to get us to take what they say seriously has less to do with either a factual look or an air of conceptual elegance than it has with their capacity to convince us that what they say is a result of their having actually penetrated (or if you prefer, having been penetrated by) another form of life, of having truly 'been there'. (Geertz, 1989, p. 58)

In 'Being There, Writing Here', an overview of the legacy of anthropology, Geertz reiterates the realisation that many of the prevailing assumptions about the validity of 'empirical scientific method' and the superiority of western culture from which anthropology emerged are no longer valid. The end of colonialism and a shift in the moral and ideological relations between the 'first' and 'third' worlds, have:

> Altered radically the nature of social relationships between those who ask and look, and those asked and looked at...(and)..the gap between engaging others where they are and representing them where they aren't - always immense but not much noticed - has become extremely visible. (Geertz, 1989, p. 60)

At the centre of this methodological crisis are questions about the nature of representation, relating to both the anthropologists' fieldwork, 'Who are 'we' to describe 'them'? Is it possible ?, What is the evidence?, How is it collected, What does it show?', and the ethnographic text, 'Who is to be persuaded? And of What?' (Geertz, 1989, p. 61).

1

Ethnographic Film Re-Presents 'Reality'

Some attempts to resolve these problems and to find new methods of study evolved out of the development of film and video technology. By the 1970s film emerged as an increasingly popular form of ethnographic representation. Ethnographic film breathed new life into anthropology, both as a new approach to field work and a reliable source of research data. The idea that 'seeing is believing' saw the presentation of direct visual evidence as a valuable addition to the rigorous scientific methods of anthropology.

One of the earliest ethnographic film-makers, Robert Gardner, held the view that the:

> evidence of documentary cinema is of a direct and unambiguous kind, being reality instantaneously captured and suffering no distortions due to faults of sight, memory or semantic interpretation. (Gardner, 1957, p. 346)

Karl Heider, a major proponent of ethnographic film's value to anthropology, maintained that, 'In ethnographic film, film is the tool and ethnography the goal' (1976, p. 4). He declined to define ethnographic film beyond that, 'which reflects ethnographic understanding' (Ibid:8) and concentrated on outlining a list of 'ethnographic attributes' which would enable one to determine the 'degree of ethnographicness' of a film. These were primarily concerned with wholeness - whole people, whole bodies, whole acts - presented in context, examined from an ethnographic viewpoint and supported by written materials.

However, this purely functional adoption of film as an ethnographic tool inherited more problems than it resolved. By coupling the conventions and techniques of classic documentary production with traditional methods of anthropology, without consideration of the related questions posed by critical film theory, ethnographic film found itself 'ill-defined' as film theorist Bill Nichols points out,

> Most often ethnographic films attempt to explain or describe some aspect of another culture to members of the film-maker's own culture within a context informed to a varying extent by traditional anthropological and ethnographic concerns and concepts and perpetuating most of their political limitations: ideology is a word seldom used

2

in studies of other cultures, and considerations of who defines culture and how (where do We draw the line around Them?) or, even more, of the ideological implications of representing one culture to another receive scant attention. (Nichols:1981:238)

As a result the viewer is led to believe that what is seen is a 'direct representation of reality' mediated only by the 'expert ethnographer' in his 'objective and scientifically informed' narration while 'the camera seems to be an invisible, completely neutral observer' (Nichols, 1981, p. 241).

By adopting the presumptions (and observational style) of Direct Cinema - that the camera is able to record events without interference and thereby offer a faithful depiction of the 'real' world - ethnographic film-makers initially ignored a number of crucial issues. Firstly, that film mediates between reality and the viewer, and secondly, that the act of filming itself alters and distorts reality; through its technical processes (framing, shot selection), in the relations of interaction between producers and subjects, and in the construction of a finished product (editing, juxtaposition of images and distortions of space and time).

Through these distortions the ethnographer's inherent ideological biases and cultural values are inevitably encoded into the completed film, through the selection of words and images and in their final combination. While some written ethnographies may acknowledge (or rationalise) their procedures of collection, selection and interpretation of material, this aspect is generally absent from ethnographic film. However, both forms of revealing one culture to another are bound in a one-way process, controlled and determined by the anthropologist and informed by the ideology of 'modern' Western positivist methods and academic discourse.

Reflexivity

We create order. We don't discover it. We organise a reality that is meaningful for us. It is around these organisations of reality that film makers construct films. (Ruby:1977:5)

In order to reveal this hidden hand and mind of the anthropologist/film-maker in ethnographic film, Jay Ruby develops the concept of 'reflexivity'. Ruby maintains that the product (film) cannot be viewed in isolation and needs to be examined in terms of a complete 'Producer-Process-Product' model. The producers (anthropologist/film-maker), 'have ethical, political, aesthetic and scientific obligations' (Ibid:9), NOT to be objective and should intentionally reveal themselves - their assumptions and methods, their decisions of selection, and production practices in the interactive process of constructing the film. For Ruby this is crucial in order to break the audience 'suspension of disbelief' and the illusion of film as a 'transparent' medium. In this way the ethnographic film-maker can move beyond the impersonal traditional documentary method, 'by exposing themselves in the same way they expose others' (Ruby, 1977, p. 8).

For Ruby, the intention of the film-maker and the methodology applied by the anthropologist is crucial to the understanding of a film and the resulting process must be incorporated into the product through 'reflexive' practice. This serves to,

> inform audiences about who they are [Anthropologist/Film-maker], and how their identities affect their films, and instruct audiences about the process of articulation from the economic, political, cultural structures and ideologies surrounding documentary to the mechanics of production (Ibid, p. 4).

This conception of 'reflexivity' can be extended as a mechanism to reveal the impact of the film crew on the situation and dissect the resultant power relations which inevitably develop between the producers and the subjects. Presumptions about the 'neutrality' of the technology of film production and the 'factual' nature of conventional documentary practice serve to isolate the production process from form and content. Often the film crew - a highly visible presence in the field - is absent from the film, leaving the impression that the events portrayed occur 'naturally' without intervention.

Tomaselli et al. point out that the 'Intrusion of ideology guides the 'lived' relation between the subjects and film crew' (1986:27), and while the adoption of 'reflexive' methods may go some way toward revealing this relation, the pervasive impact of ideology is more difficult to isolate and almost impossible to overcome. The producer/anthropologist/camera operator carry an idea of the images and 'story' to be 'captured' and seek out, recognise, and select material consistent with these pre-conceived notions and perceptions.

The Eye Of The 'Other'

A significantly different approach to the problematic that cultural bias and 'ideological intrusion' is unavoidable in the creation of a filmic representation of one culture by another, was adopted by Sol Worth and John Adair (1972). They set up an experiment with Navajo Indians to enable them to make films about themselves from their own cultural perspective, 'Films *of* a culture, rather than about a culture.'

Worth wanted to determine whether the unique cultural point of view of the Navajo would translate into a different filmic representation. Worth equated film structure with language and set out to discover whether different cultures would also construct different film forms. This hypothesis was supported to an extent although it was difficult to measure the degree of difference in representation as the films were all individual subjective creations. The films did reveal a different set of cultural codes in the composition and assemblage of images and the choice of symbolism. Of note in this experiment is the prime emphasis on the social organisation of the filming process and the focus on 'technical' instruction without any intervention with regard to technique, style, or form.

This early experiment in empowering subject-communities to express their own cultural perspective rather than be 'captured' and represented by technologically and academically qualified 'experts' has broadened the framework from which many of the new approaches to using video in subject-communities have developed. Emergent methodologies such as 'Community video', 'popular video' and 'participatory video' continue to grapple with resolving many of the same problems of representation, and unequal power relationships within the production process.

Video For The People

The editorial of an issue of *Media Development* focusing on 'Video for the people' characterises this emerging method as:

> Such video is at the intersection between education and animation, conscientisation and agitation, cultural resistance and creativity...it tries to re-create reality, but in an unusual way. It's the reality which the people themselves choose rather than the surface reality chosen for them by the mass media. In addition, it's a collective assessment of their world and worldviews. (Traber and Lee, 1989, p. 1)

'Community video' projects in South Africa have aimed at democratising video production by 'empowering' subject-communities through enabling their full participation in all stages of the production process. Many of these projects have emerged to meet political and cultural goals defined by a 'community' and are usually facilitated by outside technical expertise. However, the degree of 'community' participation in the form and content of the production varies depending on the project, and there are still many problems relating to the transfer of skills, the impact of 'facilitators' on the decision-making process, and their influence on the finished product. Despite these 'process problems' the real strength of these approaches is in their focus on production as a process and their attempts to challenge and redefine conventional production practices and relations, and thereby transfer the power to determine meaning to the subject community.

The following table of differences (Tomaselli, 1989) between community and professional video illustrates the numerous benefits to producers and subject-communities that can be achieved through adopting community video methods.

6

Community and Professional Video: Table of Differences

Community video	*Professional & conventional video*
Communication	
Group media animates and mobilises personal experience in group contexts.	Mass media informs and homogenises personal experience in individual contexts
Non-profit motive	Profit motive
Develops human relations	Develops techniques
Communication associated with process	Communication associated with technical quality
Knowledge	
Produces new knowledge	'Restricts' knowledge or repackages and reconstructs in new ways
Recovers local history	Emulates dominant view of world
Retains local cultural specificity in terms of subjects	Homogenises local cultures in terms of markets and techniques
Questions of Democracy	
Emphasises relationships	Fragments relationships
Horizontal/participative working relationships	Imposed/top-down working relationships
Transformative	Reformist
Coding	
Creates new codes, if often crude, but organic origins address community's agenda	Refines conventional styles, sophistication often hides local issues and specificities
Refers to processes beyond the community	Literal/if processes not shown they do not exist
Production, Distribution, Exhibition	
Production cannot be executed in terms of pre-determined schedules	Production must be executed in terms of pre-determined schedules
Process precedes product	Product is only goal. Process is concealed
Develops local audience	Develops national and international markets
Crew not alienated from its labour	Crew alienated from its labour
Participant video-makers are part of local distribution networks	Are alienated from their audiences through independent distribution

Continued on next page

7

Power, Empowerment

Decision-making power vested in the subject-community	Decision-making power retained and secured in the production crew and/or producers
Initial power relationships exposed and negotiated between crew and subject-community	Nature of power relationships mystified by crew in its relations with the subject-community
Empowers/active response	Disempowers/passive response
Community networks strengthened	Community networks exploited and/or weakened
Community must take responsibility for the completion of the video	Crew takes responsibility for completion of video
Facilitates both video and political theory building	Prevents theory building by concealing processes of production
Producers are part of the subject-community or are drawn into it	Producers are outside subject-community
Collective decision-making	Hierarchical decision-making
Long-term relationships between crew and community develops	Short-term relationship develops
Viewers have political expectations	Viewers want to be entertained
Empowerment takes place, if differentially, at every level of production, from production techniques to recovery of local histories and catalysation of community organisational networks	Usually only film/video-makers are empowered. Sometimes subject-communities can be detrimentally affected through exposure to alien influences and payment for acting services.

Source: Tomaselli, K.O. 'Transferring Video Skills to the Community: The problem of Power', *Media Development*, Vol. 36, No. 4, p. 13.

8

Lesotho Herders Video Project

The main production component of the *Lesotho Herders Video Project* was undertaken in 1991 as part of an 'Integrated Research' project into 'Conservation and Livestock Management in Lesotho' under the auspices of the Institute for Social and Economic Research at the University of Durban-Westville. The research is termed 'integrated' as it involved fieldwork by an anthropologist, Tim Quinlan, an ecologist, Craig Morris, two video producers, Steve Schmidt and myself, and interpreter and video production trainee, Remaketse Letlema, with the research informed by the various perspectives and perceptions of the group members.

The fieldwork consisted of three trips of about three weeks each during 1991. These were timed to enable us to capture conditions during the different seasons, i.e. Summer (26 January - 12 February), Autumn (1 - 13 April), and Winter (8 - 21 July). Each of these trips had a different focus as we developed a relationship with the herders and adapted to working under the difficult and remote conditions (see map, Appendix 1).

We ended up with a total of 26 hours of raw footage (6hrs U-matic / 3hrs Hi8 / 2 hrs Video8 / 9 hrs S-VHS / 6 hrs VHS) from which two videos have been edited. The first is a demonstration film, *MOTEBONG - Going to Lesotho to make a Film*, which was made following the first trip for screening to herders during the second trip. The second video is a short 'reflexive' look at our discussions about the film in the field. This was edited by Tim Quinlan for screening at a conference. The script of the final video and the various drafts from previous stages in the project are compiled in the Appendices.

Tomaselli et al. (1986, p. 37) offer an expanded 'Producer-Process-Product' model as a framework for both analysis of existing ethnographic film and as an outline of areas for consideration in developing a working method to approach ethnographic film work. This model includes the following relationships: (INTENTION) - Anthropologist - Producer - Process - Subjects - Audience - (PURPOSE). This provides a more comprehensive model with which to examine the progression of the *Lesotho Herders Video Project* as it is the nature of these relationships that informed the process and ultimately created the product.

Intention

Anthropologist

The three main objectives of the project (as outlined by project leader Tim Quinlan in his 1990 application for research funds from University of Durban-Westville) were:

> ...to produce an integrated ecological/sociological analysis of livestock and range management practices in Lesotho. Secondly, the intent is to provide critical knowledge in a field where such knowledge is very limited, in order to develop current understanding of ecological processes in the Maluti/Drakensburg region. Thirdly the intent is to communicate the research product through both literature and video which will provide a substantial basis for further research ... the proposed research will embody a historical dimension which is critical to the understanding of ecological processes ... A core feature of the proposed research is the documentation of data on video. While the proposed research is exploratory in terms of seeking to truly integrate natural and social scientific research, it is also experimental in terms of seeking to produce videos which facilitate communication of scientific results and which are of educational value. In short the research plan is to be innovative in research methodology and in communication of research results.

Outlining the methodology and fieldwork procedure to be adopted Quinlan says:

> ... findings will be assessed with stock owners and herders by means of the anthropologist's research method of participant observation ... The video producers will design film plans on the basis of the research plan of the ecologist and the anthropologist. These will then be discussed and assessed by the research team. Skeleton schedules of topics, foci and particular footage will be drawn up so that *all the researchers will be aware of how the videos will be made and the content they should include.* (My emphasis)

11

Quinlan (1990) further outlines the proposed role of the video producers and their relationship with the researchers:

> The key for success here is the provision of several skeleton film plans which allow for both systematic filming and flexibility for modification, according to particular conditions encountered whilst in the field. Flexibility is the core concern in design of this part of the research. Although the videos will be based on the studies of the anthropologist and the ecologist, the video producers have an important role of experimenting to find the best ways of communicating scientific knowledge through the powerful medium of video. An important proviso of the research design here is that video production cannot simply be a visual record of academic study. As professional communicators, the video producers will be influential in seeing and interpreting events in the field, thereby challenging and supplementing the observations of the other two researchers. In turn the producers will promote insight into ecological processes under study. Moreover, through the interaction of all the researchers, the whole group will be drawn into experimenting with the question of how to most effectively communicate research results on video.

Quinlan acknowledges that much of this initial proposal was 'impression management' aimed at convincing the university to provide the additional funds needed to undertake the video project, and as such it is not a true reflection of his working concept of the video. I use this example of his research proposal as an illustration of the common conception amongst academics of video as product, which can only be justified in terms of 'educational and research' purposes to facilitate communication of scientific results which are of an educational value. This echoes Heider's proposal that film is merely a 'tool' in the service of academic 'science'.

Producers
Apart from the realisation that flexibility is a core concern many of the other production guidelines such as 'video producers will design film plans ... which allow for both systematic filming...', and 'all the

researchers will be aware of how the films will be made and the content they should include', were rejected as unrealistic in pre-production planning (and impossible to implement in the field). We decided to draw on community video approaches and attempt to facilitate herder participation in the project. We recognised that the production procedures we adopted and the process of interaction with the subject-community would to a large degree determine the content of our source material, and ultimately define the product. We were all aware of the shortcomings of standard BBC 'Natural History' type documentary production which was concerned primarily with product and operated to a set production formula - presenting a pre-constructed argument supported by selected excerpts from interviews and visual overlay. We wanted to avoid this deterministic method (characterised as Professional and conventional video in the Table on pages 7-8).

We also acknowledged that our presence and all our equipment was likely to have a great impact on the situation of interaction. While this could not be entirely eliminated we planned to document this interaction with a second camera and include this 'reflexive' perspective in the final video both as an acknowledgement of our presence and a 'self-conscious' view of our interaction with the herders.

This use of 'reflexive' methods to reveal our production practices and interaction with the subject-community was a central concern of the producers and seen as a crucial component of both the process and the product.

Process

We decided to focus on a process which would attempt to capture and represent the herders' 'lifestyle' as seen from their point of view. It was therefore agreed that we would adopt a more open and interactive approach which would enable herder 'participation' and allow them, as much as possible, to determine the overall content of the video.

The main objective in overcoming the divide between 'us' and 'them', the observers and the observed, was to shift our role from instigators to facilitators in the filming process. We hoped to create, through interaction with the herders, a forum for discussion which would allow the herders to reveal their own understandings of their conditions of existence and explore their current concerns and hopes for the future. We realised this was a problematic proposition and our attempts to find mechanisms to achieve this became the main emphasis of the production process.

The Intended Subject

The herders are largely young men and boys who live and tend livestock at cattleposts situated in the remote mountain region of North-Eastern Lesotho. Most of them are hired - at a rate of between eight and twelve sheep per year - while some are sons of stock owners. They endure a very basic existence, surviving on a diet of mainly maizemeal 'pap' and water, supplemented by sheep's milk in summer and occasionally meat from stock that die. The cattleposts are rudimentary stone huts and kraals spread out along the many valleys within the designated common grasslands. The areas are divided into 'summer cattleposts' in the alpine

The two young herders who sang and recited praise poems for us.

zone and 'winter cattleposts' in the sub-alpine valleys. We intended to reveal the lifestyles of the herders and their conditions of work, as well as explore issues relating to livestock management and the conservation of the alpine grasslands. While the herders were our central subject, we also intended to record the opinions of stock owners and range management officials, and contextualise the herders within the livestock economy of Lesotho.

Audience & Pre-Conceptions Of Product
At the outset the pre-conceptions of the type of video we were aiming at varied. The difficulty in deciding on the form the final product would take was linked to an uncertainty about which audience the video was aimed at. This was a result of our differing objectives. There was much initial debate over the final form of the video and the target audience as we realised that there was potential for a number of videos to emerge from the project and that we would each probably produce very different videos given our different areas of concern and focus. However, due to the 'integrated' nature of the project it was necessary to synthesise our different areas of interest and resolve differences. Our later experiences in the field, given our production practices, were to a large extent, to determine both the final form and content of the video.

Producers

Anthropologist and researcher Tim Quinlan initially saw the video as complementing his research into livestock management in the alpine zone. While his research was primarily focused on the use of cattleposts, livestock management and herding methods, he saw the video as a valuable source of visual material which would be useful for contextualising the research. This would be used as an adjunct to the research findings, both as part of presentations to other academics and as an input and an intervention into the Lesotho government's Range Management Programme. This focus later centred on a form of 'advocacy' video which would provide a 'voice' for herder's concerns.

The University of Durban-Westville Video Producer, Steve Schmidt, was primarily concerned with obtaining 'high-quality' source material which would also allow the option of producing an additional 'professional' documentary for possible broadcast as a means of generating further funds for the project. While agreeing with the need to develop an 'interactive process', the product still remained an important emphasis as he felt 'In order to get more money to make more films you have to make 'good' films and so we need to direct our film to a certain audience'.

As co-producer I assisted with the production of the main video, and was interested in using a second camera to record the process and interaction between the film crew and the herders. This 'reflexive' component of the video was to be incorporated into the final video. In addition, I hoped to produce a complete 'reflexive' video examining the process of making the herder video.

Ecologist Craig Morris wanted to document the different types of vegetation and the state of wetland areas as an on-going visual record. It was suggested that this could best be done photographically. However, it was felt that video was also needed to show the relation between people and their environment. Herders would also be interviewed on their attitudes to conservation measures and on how they used natural resources. Again this would form part of the Herder video with the possible expansion into a 'conservation' video.

Videos By And For Anthropologists

Quinlan had edited two videos from footage recorded on two different field trips undertaken during his previous research in 1988. These were entitled *Cattleposts and herders in Lesotho* (1989) and *Doing Fieldwork: An anthropologist in the field* (1989). Both reflect Tomaselli's observation that 'video technology directs producers down ideologically predictable paths' (1989, p. 12).

Cattleposts and herders in Lesotho covered the same subject matter as the video we aimed to produce. It uses an 'African' narrator to provide an 'authentic' feel consistent with the visual content (male, African, herders) and lend credibility to the narration. The narration, in English, is supported by various images of herder activities and the way of life in Lesotho. The commentary is also quite dense and academic, filled with facts and figures about the region and the herders, and an overview of the socio-economic significance of the livestock economy. Quinlan also appears on camera on location and at the University of Durban-Westville as an 'expert' supporting his own written narrative.

The herders themselves are merely a visual presence, while their lifestyle and conditions of existence are described by the narrator and by Quinlan the herders sit in the background and look on. The only herder that speaks for himself says two sentences in English in reply to questions from Quinlan. There is also one other interview in Sesotho, with an English voice-over by Quinlan translating the discussion. This segment repeats what the narrator has just told us, and then Quinlan appears on screen to make the point again. Another social anthropologist is also used as an 'authority' to relate the Sotho herders' lifestyle to herders in other parts of the world and to point out the significance of Quinlan's research.

The opening sequence, which shows Tim holding a microphone and asking various people (men, women, children) whether they would like to go to the cattleposts), has a slight 'reflexive' feel, but the camera remains an invisible presence throughout the video, only discerned through the reaction of subjects, who stop to observe the observer. The video also uses mood music to invoke, drama, tranquillity and a sense of activity. The closing sequence uses an array of special effects as we see herders in mosaic, freeze frame and strobes. We see a depersonalised view of the herders as 'objects of study' and a component of a broader 'livestock economy'. They are powerless to respond or contribute to their representation.

An Anthropologist in the field takes the form of a 'reflexive' video (mainly in content) as it examines the methods of anthropology in general as well as the specific conditions and difficulties faced by

17

Quinlan in conducting his research in Lesotho. It is very revealing and insightful about its subject matter and subject (Tim Quinlan), and includes critical analysis of the concepts it discusses. However, the video conforms to dominant documentary conventions of exposition with a narrator supported by Tim providing 'in the field' and 'in the office' presentations to camera for continuity and to relate theory to practice (Tim explains that a woman was chosen as a narrator to off-set gender bias - using a woman as a voice of authority shows that women are also anthropologists).

Although the presence of the camera is acknowledged it is only slightly revealed, and while we gain a sense of Tim's intimacy with the cameraman, the operator remains invisible. The video opens with Tim saying to camera, "Making a film on Lesotho is itself an eye-opener, learning to visualise ethnographic data made me look anew at familiar situations and aspects to daily village life". The narrator says, "This film is based on fieldwork done by Tim Quinlan in the classical tradition". Towards the end of the video the narrator mentions that, "Shooting a film raises ethical questions", and we see a man talking to Tim turn toward the camera and ask "Is it a photo?". In another revealing sequence we see Tim approach a group of small children torn between curiosity and terror, he says "Shoota filim", and moves towards them with a microphone, causing them to retreat and huddle together.

Both of these films were primarily made for academic use, for anthropology students and conference presentations. In this context the reflexive component of the second one complements the first. A hybrid of the two would create a composite 'reflexive' film, in Ruby's terms, as in the first the herders are the subject of Tim's study and in the second he studies himself and reveals his methods. However, while Quinlan brings life to his examination of anthropological method through personification and exerts almost total control over his representation (as instigator-producer-process-subject), the 'other' subjects in his films are depersonalised and presented as mere objects of study. This is highlighted by the use of freeze frames, which although a pleasant and effective visual effect, make the subjects (already without a voice) unable even to act and 'captured' by technology.

Quinlan acknowledged the shortcomings in these videos and wanted to avoid the 'expert in the field' impression they gave and their producer-centric bias of presenting 'subjects as objects'. We were looking for ways of breaking down the barriers of culture, language and

18

power, between the production team and the herders and to find mechanisms to enable the herders to speak for themselves.

Language Barriers

One of the major barriers to achieving the aim of herder self-expression was that of language. Quinlan's previous films used mainly English interviews and English narration as they were aimed at an English-speaking audience. This limited the number of interviews that could be used to those herders who could speak some English. Most of the interaction between Quinlan and the herders consisted of straight questions and answers with Quinlan leading discussion. This was something we hoped to avoid as we sought to achieve a dialogue within groups of herders that would allow them to express their own opinions.

*Chuck Scott and Steve Schmidt recording
a group discussion in Jareteng*

Tim and Steve had made a feasibility trip in the winter of 1990 to get some idea of the practicalities of undertaking a video production in the remote cattleposts in the alpine region. One of the major problems to emerge from this trip was the inadequacy of Quinlan's Sesotho:

> While I could converse adequately with the herders, the inevitable stumbles in speech, questions to clarify words, nuances and slang, are disruptions which do not come across well on video. In particular I struggled with allegorical statements in descriptions of environmental issues, as well as with explaining the concept of video to many herders, who have limited if any experience of it. (1991, p. 8)

Tim planned to overcome this language barrier by hiring a Sotho to conduct interviews and to be trained in the use of video equipment and production techniques.

Process

The following description of our field work takes the form of an ethnography, though not necessarily informed by ethnographic understanding, but rather my personal experience and reflections on the production process. In keeping with this informal feel I will also change to a more personal style of using the first names of participants.

Trip 1: Exploratory Phase

Tim Quinlan had established a base camp at Mapholaneng thirty kilometres inland from the capital of the Mokhotlong District in Northeastern Lesotho. He had been staying here with the Alotsi family during his Ph.d research in 1986-88 and we were offered accommodation

Remaketse Letlema

in the main hut on the three-hut homestead.

Our arrival in January 1991 created quite a stir in the small village surrounding the homestead and there was always a crowd of children and older boys as well as regular visits from women and older men. However, Tim was well known in the area and many people came to greet him and inquire about what he was doing. We discovered that there was no Sotho word for 'film' and explaining the concept of 'capturing images on magnetic tape' and 'constructing a video representation of herder lifestyles' was not easy as Tim only spoke conversational Sotho.

A Sotho called Champane Champane had agreed to join us as interviewer and interpreter on the trip, but when we arrived we found that he had gone to the capital Maseru. This was the first of many setbacks on the first trip. However, we met a young man, Remaketse Letlama (who Tim considered a likely candidate), in a local restaurant. After explaining what we were doing (making a video about herders) we asked him if he would like to join us. He was very keen and after an interview with his father, where we had to explain what we were doing and how Remaketse would benefit from the experience, it was agreed that he would become our interviewer/trainee.

Remaketse turned out to be an ideal addition to the production crew as he had worked as a herder during his school vacations and was familiar with the area. We discovered that he also had a keen interest in film and owned a 16mm projector which he used to screen films at the local bar - when he could find films and spare globes for the projector. Remaketse had also worked in the mines in Welkom for three years and all in all typified much of the common experience of young Sotho men.

We realised that Remaketse would play an important role in our interaction with the herders and we spent a great deal of time discussing issues we hoped would emerge out of the video with him. These related to the relationship between the herders and the general socio-economic conditions in Lesotho. We wanted to find answers to questions like why do young boys herd rather than attend school. Do they choose the isolation and hardships of the cattle posts rather than the relatively easy-going and sociable village life? What their hopes and aspiration were. How they felt about life in the mountains. We also wanted to reveal their understanding of environmental, livestock and grazing issues, and how the Lesotho government's range management policy affected them.

Although Quinlan had been conducting research in Lesotho since 1988 and had recorded some VHS material on three prior field trips, the

Remaketse Letlema

four-man production team and much larger amount of equipment created a number of logistical difficulties that took almost a week to resolve on the first trip.

Equipment

We had opted for S-VHS equipment as a compromise between quality and portability and had hired a VCR which docked onto our main camera. The second camera was a standard VHS camcorder. However, this quest for 'quality' source material led us to try low-band U-matic, Hi8 and Video8 equipment on subsequent trips. We also carried a small portable colour monitor (12 x 20 cm) which proved invaluable for 'screenings' and reviewing material. Vital accessories like batteries, chargers, tripods, microphones, cables, etc. made up the bulk of the equipment. In order to recharge our batteries in the field we had bought a small generator which required that we carry about 15 litres of fuel. We had special saddlebags made up to carry the equipment. The idea was that two donkeys would carry the four packs as it was felt that horses could not be trusted with the equipment as they had a tendency to bolt if startled. Tim had calculated the weight a donkey could carry on the basis of one 50 kg bag of maize and concluded that 40 - 50 kg of equipment per pack animal should be possible when distributed into two evenly balanced saddlebags.

However, after two false starts we discovered that neither the saddlebags nor our donkeys could stand up to the weight of the equipment. In addition the summer rains had flooded the rivers and we were unable to take our planned route into the mountains. This left us stranded in Mapholaneng for a week as we repaired the saddle bags and tried to find a stronger donkey or preferably a mule. We ended up having to use one of the horses as a pack animal to carry the bulk of the equipment.

Village Video

This setback turned out to be a useful period for introducing Remaketse to the equipment while videoing around the village.

We had been documenting the loading of pack animals and the preparations for our departure when we noticed a large group of people working on a hillside opposite the homestead. It turned out that this was a 'food for work' scheme where people help combat soil erosion in the fields and are paid in maize and other basic food supplies. We saw this as fitting into the conservation video and recorded people filling a donga with rocks and interviewed the local organiser. At the end of the day the women ululated, sang and danced. It was difficult to tell to what extent this was in response to the presence of the camera.

In order to use our time productively we decided to drive through to Mokhotlong and interview the head of the Teba mine recruitment office. Remaketse had told us that a lot of Sothos were being sent back from the mines and that very few new mine workers were being recruited. We thought this could tie in with the herder video as it further limited the number of employment opportunities available to young men in Lesotho. This interview, conducted in Sotho by Tim and Remaketse, took the form of straight questions and answers around the availability of work on the mines in South Africa and the number of jobs available to Sotho workers in the area.

Right Place, Wrong Time

On our first attempt to drive through to Mokhotlong we were unable to cross a flooded bridge. Steve wanted to stay and see if anyone would try and cross so that we could video it and capture some 'dramatic footage'. After waiting to see if the water level would subside we decided to return to Mapholaneng. We returned the next day to find that a Mercedes truck had been washed off the bridge the previous afternoon and that the driver and a passenger had drowned. We also heard that a horseman had been washed away and drowned. Steve commented that we should have waited and would have been able to film these disasters.

This was the first of many situations illustrating the enticement to capture 'events' or 'happenings' when you are travelling with video equipment. There were other occasions when there was some disagreement as to whether or not a particular situation was worth recording and the person proposing the shoot would have to justify its necessity in relation to the overall concept of the video. Often circumstances such as the distance that needed to be covered on that day, or whether we really wanted to unload, unpack, set-up, shoot, pack, collect the animals, reload - ultimately determined whether or not we filmed en route. We were often faced with practical considerations as production determinants - above aesthetic or functional imperatives.

Screenings
We had also been recording general activity around the village; women collecting water, men feeding horses, children playing etc., and we started screening the day's footage on the monitor in the evenings. This became a very popular event and would be attended by some thirty people. Although this was purely for entertainment it was also an ideal way of illustrating to the villagers what we were doing. This resulted in people calling us to video other activities. For example our host, Ntate Tanki Alotsi, would approach us, mimic holding a video camera, say 'shoota' and beckon us to follow him. On one occasion it turned out his wife was grinding maize and he wanted us to video this. He also told us that the 'food for work' team were receiving their food supplies and suggested we record this, having seen our footage of the workers (which included his wife).

The screenings also demonstrated that people found pleasure in seeing themselves and others on screen. The monitor was very small (12x20cm) yet viewers would identify people only a few centimetres high on screen and point them out, call out their names in recognition, with much amusement. We also recorded these screenings and the audience response. Although the majority of the viewers, women and children, would have had very little, if any, experience of viewing videos or TV, they may have seen the occasional films screened at the local restaurant. However, their pleasure and interest in watching our footage was stimulated by the recognition of people they knew (and themselves) and a sense of identification. This served to promote a willingness (and pride) amongst people in the village to be recorded and overcome any suspicions (as to our presence, motives, and activities) that may have existed.

On The Path

The heavy rains, flooded rivers, and trouble with the donkeys and saddlepacks made progress slow and laborious and the +-35 kms to the first winter cattleposts at Khotlo Inja (Neck of the Dogs) took three days. By this stage the adventure of experiencing the life of mountain men had worn off and fatigue had set in. When we finally reached the cattleposts, the herders gave us a warm welcome and promptly slaughtered a goat for us. Before we were aware of what was happening Remaketse said, "This is something you should film". However, it happened so quickly there wasn't enough time to set up the equipment and there was very little light as it was dusk. It took the herders under ten minutes to skin the goat and cut it up. We thought that we would have plenty of other opportunities to capture this occurrence (as it turned out we had to reconstruct it as one of our final shoots at the end of the second trip). It also raised questions as to whether or not we should have asked them to wait until we could set up a camera, but it was felt we should only to capture events as they happened 'naturally' and avoid creating situations so we could film them.

The next morning we awoke somewhat relieved at having reached a cattlepost, though thoroughly exhausted. I was recording a herder milking sheep for breakfast. He was aware of my presence and after looking directly at the camera and smiling, continued his activity with deliberation. Another herder also seemed to want to be recorded and set about deftly catching a sheep and proceeding to milk it.

At this point I asked a disgruntled looking Steve how he felt to finally have reached a cattlepost, his response to camera was "Well its misty and raining again, looks like another shit day riding in the rain. I've really had enough of horses and donkeys. I think the next trip we must insist that the film-makers get dropped off here by helicopter and then picked up and taken to the next place. For artistic temperament to function properly we need to be comfortable and well rested". This half-joking response reflected our frustration at the substantial effort required

26

to transport and set-up the equipment. Much of our time had been spent loading and unloading the horses and donkeys. As a result we kept the camcorder handy for video recording of cattle posts and scenery while we moved between posts but were hesitant to unload the bulk of the equipment due to the amount of time and effort involved.

Accidental Encounters

Our next video-contact with herders a day later turned out to be an 'accidental encounter'. We awoke at our camp to discover that one of our horses had disappeared. Tim and Remaketse rode off to try and find it, while Steve and I sorted out the equipment and charged batteries. We set up the main camera and were taking scenic shots of cattleposts in the surrounding valleys. A group of six herders arrived, obviously interested in our presence and what we were doing. Our dependency on Tim and Remaketse for communication became exceedingly apparent.

Apart from the greeting 'Khotso Ntate' neither of us could speak Sotho. Steve volunteered 'Shoota Filim' but this didn't seem any significant advance in communication. We decided to screen footage we had shot at the other cattle post as a way of showing what we were doing. Although outdoor daytime screenings were not ideal on the small monitor, it was our only mechanism for communication - visually. Before we had time to develop this experiment in visual communication Tim and Remaketse returned (without the horse) and after some discussion with the herders they agreed to be interviewed. We then linked the monitor to the camera for direct playback and I set up the camcorder on a wide shot to capture the whole scene. At this point, Steve who was operating the main camera prompted Remaketse, "OK we're rolling this interview, ask them who they are, where they come from and all that kind of stuff, get into it slowly" (We ultimately chose this shot as our opening sequence in the final edit as it clearly illustrated how our process started out. In contrast the later video encounters reveal how far we had progressed in enabling our subjects to speak for themselves and determine the content of the video). Considering that this was Remaketse's first field interview with a group of herders he showed considerable skill in adopting a conversational approach to introducing questions and maintaining a relaxed atmosphere.

At this point discussion is still very much carried by Remaketse. An example from the transcript:

R: How do you entertain yourself?

Herder: There's nothing besides herding.

R: Is there any work you want besides herding?

H: Many, and I like farming very much.

R: What about a job from the mines or at camp?

H: I've been working at the mines and I still want work at the mines but the problem is that people are coming home and it's very hard to get work at the mines

R: Have you been to school?

H: No.

R: Is it because you didn't like it or because your parents didn't have the means to send you?

H: My parents didn't have the means

R: How many sheep are you herding?

H: Quite a lot

R: Are they increasing or decreasing?

H: They are dying

R: Where do you herd them?

H: Around here

R: Do you stay here the whole time?

H: Since I have been here I've stayed here one year and six months without going home

R: Don't you miss your girlfriends

H: (Laughs) No.

Much of the initial discussion was in this vein but when it came to issues affecting the herders they were slightly more forthcoming.

R: Do you think in the future the stock will increase and what of the grazing?

H1: The stock is decreasing and the land is diminishing.

H2: The population is increasing and everybody wants to rear stock so in future land will diminish and stock decrease because we will not have a space to graze.

This last statement, though prompted by a question from Remaketse, sums up what was to emerge as one of the herders' central concerns. It also supported the thrust of the research findings. However, we hoped to move beyond this realisation of problems to some suggested solutions.

It turned out our missing stallion had run off with a herd of mares and the rest of the day was spent trying to recover it. This would have made great footage had any of us been able to record it, but we were too concerned with trying to catch the horse.

Cattleposts

At the next post we came across a young boy playing a Sekhankula (a musical instrument resembling a violin, made from a 5 Litre oil can with wire strings and played with a horse hair bow). We asked him if we could film him playing it. He declined, saying he was not good enough and that we should wait for the other herder who was a better musician. He was also probably intimidated by our arrival. The other herder arrived and agreed to play for us. This sequence turned out to have a very 'natural' feel as the music performance followed on from a discussion with Remaketse. Once the herder adjusted to the presence of the camera he appeared to become much more at ease and 'unaware' of the camera. We played back the interview and the performance and he seemed very pleased.

The following interaction was with a man and his two young sons. They boys watched the interview being relayed to the monitor as we spoke to the father. We had generally decided to set up the camera to record the situation rather than positioning the interview to suit the camera. As a consequence this interview is visually very poor as the father is obscured by Remaketse. We then spoke to the boys who were still shy and unresponsive. We then asked them if they would like to sing. They did so after their father encouraged them. Following the song the elder boy broke into a praise poem which surprised even his father.

Another herder arrived saying he was a lesiba player (a long stick with a horsehair that is played something like a mouth organ). We asked him if he could play for us he agreed and swiftly darted up the mountainside to fetch his instrument. We then recorded this and he explained how the instrument was made and played (at Steve's request as he felt it would be useful for the Music Department at the university).

The next cattlepost was deserted but we were approached firstly by an old man and later by two young boys who played Sekhankula for us. The old herder was the only negative response we had to playing back an interview. When he saw and heard himself on the monitor he turned away and went and sat a few metres from us, showing no further interest in the video. The two boys on the other hand thoroughly enjoyed the playback of their music. They also handled the camcorder (with my assistance) and filmed one another playing music. We then looped the monitor directly to the camera enabling the herders to observe themselves being observed by the camera, while we recorded this experience with the camcorder. This enabled us to record the herders' realisation of the 'real time' of video. This encounter was similar to a person seeing himself in a mirror for the first time, though mediated by a complex system of technology. The one herder was smoking and when seeing himself smoking on the monitor blew out a large cloud of smoke to make the connection that what he was seeing was what he was doing 'here and now'. At this realisation he retreated slightly and relayed his discovery to his friend. They then both moved in closer, amused by their mutual self-recognition.

One of the two sekhankula players

Visual Treatment

The fact that the majority of the interviews and discussions were conducted in Sotho alienated the 'producers' from direct communication with the herders and left us with predominantly technical responsibilities. Our tasks included setting up and packing away equipment and ensuring that shots were in focus, correctly exposed and colour balanced, and that the sound levels were OK.

The rifle mike we were using was about half a metre long and encased in a grey-housing and windsock. This gave it an appearance of a small rocket launcher. Consequently we were afraid it might be intimidating, but many of the herders seemed to realise its function and would move toward it when they spoke. It was also impossible to keep out of shot and we decided to let the interviews proceed without direction for the camera.

As a result much of the footage shows a group of people (including Tim and Remaketse) sitting around having a discussion with the mike featuring prominently. I am often seen walking into shot with the camcorder. We also varied the shots to allow for cutaways, mostly to a medium shot to retain the interaction between the interviewer and person being interviewed. There are very few extreme close-ups of peoples faces while they are talking (this was very useful when we finally had to add sub-titles).

We had also realised the difficulties inherent in one of the central questions in ethnographic film, whether the event recorded would have occurred without the presence of the camera. Besides the theoretical paradox of whether it is possible to evaluate this proposition, our intent had been to engage with herders, and as a consequence we were responsible for initiating the form of this contact. We further played a leading role in prompting discussion. However, within this interaction there were 'activities' that formed part of routine daily occurrences that we were able to record. This was to a large degree dependent on timing and whether the camera was set up and ready to record. It also required recognition of the occurrence and a conscious decision to record it. Thus selection of material was determined both by subjective selection and technical availability. While we had decided to avoid reconstructing activities, the recording of musical performances needed to be structured to ensure 'good' sound recording, and as a result these were performances for camera. As we had decided to use only music 'indigenous' to the region in the final video the recording of music was a production criteria.

Evaluation: First Trip

On the balance the recorded material was more about 'us' than 'them'. This was mainly due to the delays at the start of the trip which resulted in us not reaching the main summer posts at Langalabelele where Tim knew more herders. We had ended up with lot of 'reflexive' footage, much of which was very revealing about our attitudes and the process we were engaged in. A great deal of this material was included in the demonstration video we edited following this trip. This reflected our concern with documenting and evaluating our interaction with the herders and our self-conscious approach. In this sense we had become our own subjects of study.

We had also not worked to any clear production plan of whom we were going to interview where. Most of the recorded interaction had taken place either with the herders at whichever cattlepost we camped at, or through us being approached by curious groups of herders. In this sense the video recordings had evolved out of more casual social interaction and as much a desire by the herders to know what we were doing as our intent to document their lifestyle.

We realised we had adopted a 'naive' approach to engaging the herders, but saw it as a valuable learning experience. While we were guided by the broad principles of 'community video' to democratise our production practices, we were not working to any clearly defined method. So while we were experienced practitioners (in video production and research respectively) we were novices at implementing our intended process in this context. As a result we were refining our interactive techniques through experiential and experimental practice. We had developed a more realistic understanding of the working conditions, and the problems of overcoming the language and communication barrier. The 'producers' had only a vague idea of what had been discussed in the interviews (related by Tim and Remaketse) and were only able to evaluate the visual content of the footage on a technical and aesthetic basis. Remaketse had also developed his own production and interaction skills. As he adapted to his role within the production team he was reaching his own understanding of where the video was going - and definitely had a clearer idea of the content of the interviews than we did.

Here are some extracts from a recording of a group discussion on our impressions of the first trip:

Remaketse: "Our trip was very educational to me. I gained a lot of experience, using the camera, learning how it worked and doing filming".

On his role of interviewer he, "Found it great, but difficult to ask

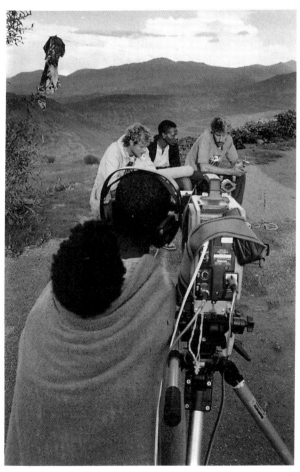

The observers observed.
Tanki' s daughter records our reflection on the first trip

questions that were not answered the way I wanted them answered".

On the reaction of people to the production crew: "Some people in the mountains got frightened as I saw them, but as we played the monitor for them some of them got interested and they will be happy to see you again and themselves on the screen. The one old man was frightened as he was not used to such things and it was completely new to him".

Tim: "I underestimated the problems of transporting the equipment and taking expensive and not very portable equipment into very rugged terrain. I was also concerned about the intrusion of the camera on a part of society where the lifestyle is very simple, but I think that we introduced it in a fairly sensitive way. It's a matter of how you do it. I did notice a difference in approach where the cameraman moves in close to a situation while the anthropologist stands back to see the whole picture".

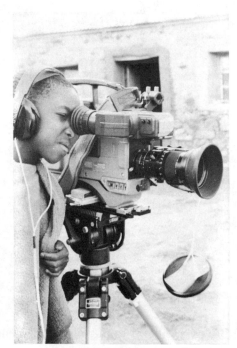

Our host Ntate Alotsi's daughter
views a reflexive discussion in Mapholaneng

Steve felt that "using the monitor to constantly play back what we had shot to show the herders themselves and what we were doing makes a big difference".

Tim replied "I'm not sure that validates our argument at all. It simply serves our own reflexive approach and interests. I'm not sure that we have communicated effectively yet what we are doing. I think it helps people to get an idea when we play back with the monitor, but its only part of the process and not the answer yet. I think when we bring back an edited film and discuss it with the herders and see what their reactions are then, we may have communicated what we are doing, and we would have done it in the right way".

We had also realised the need to overcome the dual difficulty of communicating the concept of video generally, and the objectives of the herder film specifically. Besides the 'reflexive' reviewing of footage with the monitor we had not achieved our aim of enabling the herders to 'speak for themselves' to any meaningful degree. We consequently saw a demonstration video as the means to achieving this end.

Demonstration Video
The demonstration video was edited by Steve and proved an invaluable tool for stimulating debate amongst herders.

The content of the video establishes the context of the project and researchers from the University of Durban-Westville. It traces the crew travelling to Lesotho, the journey into the mountains and subsequent interaction and interviews with herders we had recorded on the first trip. Ultimately it reflects the introspection of the producers towards their work as well as revealing our power of manipulation over the imagery and content.

The video opens with a shot of Steve filming a group of herders over which the title 'MATEBONG - Going to Lesotho to make a film' is superimposed. The opening sequence starts with a performance by Sipho Mchunu's Zulu band recorded at the University and the music track continues into helicopter shots of Durban's beach front, the harbour, the University of Durban-Westville (with titles) and a student protest march. There follows a series of walk-in shots - into Tim's office where he is seen working on a computer, then into the edit suite where we see Steve editing the video. It then cuts to a truck climbing the Sani Pass. A zoom out from the Lesotho flag finds us at the Sani Top border post. At this point another title (Lesotho) is dropped in followed by a travelling sequence in our 4x4 vehicle to Mapulaneng. At this point the music changes (to a local band recorded on an earlier trip by Steve) with general shots of village life (including a strobe effect on a young girl dancing). The next sequence sees the crew preparing to leave for the mountains and showing some of the difficulties we experienced loading animals and crossing rivers. The music shifts to the haunting melancholic strains of the sekhankula signifying the transition into the mountains. This is followed by excerpts of herder interviews, the two boys singing and the sekhankula players. The final cut sees Steve in the edit room finishing the video and switching off the machinery (and the video) with a fade to black.

While the video provided an overview of where we came from, what we do, what we had done and were doing in Lesotho, it also included a lot of icons constructed by and for a 'visually literate' viewer, such as the titles, location signs and other images linking the shifts of context and location. It also communicated (intentionally?) the power of the producer in the construction of a video. As a result it is primarily about 'our' reflexive experience of the first trip. However, the herders speak for themselves without narrative prompts and in the context of the crews interaction with them.

Once More Unto The Mountains

2. Interactive/Participatory Phase

On the second trip in April 1991 we reached the Summer Cattleposts at Langalabelele very quickly compared with the first trip. By driving the equipment through to Mateanong while Tim and Remaketse rode the horses and donkeys from Mapholaneng we saved two days travelling time.

Interactive Video

We had brought along the 40 minute rough edit of the earlier footage which we aimed to use as a catalyst or 'trigger' video to stimulate discussion and raise issues. We had found it difficult to break the question and answer routine on the first trip where we had to draw information out of the herders. Our ideal was to have them relate their experiences and voice concerns they considered important without prompting and probing. Through the use of the demonstration video we had shifted from our initial approach of interaction (interviews) and reflection (playback) to a more active (though less direct) intervention.

We informed all the herders we met en route that we were going to show the video we were making at a certain cattle post the next morning. A large group arrived and we had to have two screenings - attended by total of between twenty and thirty herders ranging in age from over seventy to under ten. The initial response was very positive:

Tsietsie: We have seen beautiful people, donkeys been loaded, people playing Sekhankula

R: Not necessarily what you have seen but did it appeal to you?

T: Yes, I saw it well

Mashaile: Yes we see it as a good thing and it appeals to us. Truly, it appeals to us and we are happy, all of us here.

Another herder adds: Even me, it appeals to me.

These responses have more to do with a pleasure of recognition and sense of identity than with a real understanding of why we were making the video and what we hoped to achieve in terms of representing herder life.

Following the screening we recorded a group discussion amongst the herders. Remaketse still played the part of interviewer, but more as a

37

facilitator in leading discussion, rather than having to draw information out of people, as discussion was much more forthcoming. One limitation, in terms of filming this situation, was the size of the group as they were spread out over ten meters and the sound quality was erratic as it was difficult to anticipate who would speak next. There was also a dynamic between the herders as the young boys appeared shy and reserved in the presence of the older herders. A group of teenagers, who were in the majority, were impatient to show that they could 'sing and play music better' than the herders they had seen in the video. Mashaile, says early on in the discussion, "After the talking we would like to sing Sotho songs and after that we will end up making poems".

For the next fifty minutes the group discussed many of the issues facing them, the deteriorating grasslands, the increasing stock numbers, difficulties of existence, government policy on stock tax and restricting grazing. Much of this discussion was extremely fruitful and the debate produced a number of different views. The group then decided they had enough of talking and said they wanted to sing. This was followed by Mashaile presenting a praise poem. The situation rapidly escalated into something of a 'cultural day' with herders taking turns to play *Lesiba* and *Sekhankula* while others danced. Activity then shifted to a demonstration of stick fighting which was fairly short-lived due to the over-exuberance of some of the participants and a number of telling blows. One herder started doing handstands and headsprings and Tim suggested we stop filming so as to not encourage him. The teenage boys had definitely become very excited and stimulated by the occasion. We also had opportunities to record a number of herder activities, spinning wool, knitting hats, general herding activity, (and in the evening) counting and checking the flock.

This trial screening was undoubtedly a great success in that it achieved its aim of generating herder response and discussion. The group experience had prompted many of the herders to respond to points made by others. The interaction had made them examine and explore their own situation in a way they had perhaps not done before. The gathering also attracted the attention of other herders and groups of two and three arrived on horseback or on foot throughout the morning. This approach formed the basis for most of the material we gathered on this trip.

Following the initial exuberance of the larger group we recorded a number of individual responses from herders. The first with an old man, Ntate Thaole Pela, who was in his seventies and had known the area since the 1930s. He recalled the history of the area in ten minutes of uninterrupted dialogue, providing good material on the deteriorating state of the grasslands.

We also recorded the 'life-story' of 23-year-old Mashaile Kapa (Appendix 2). He spoke fluently for over ten minutes without questioning (a significant advance on the average of ten word responses we had elicited on our first trip). He talked about many of the issues we had hoped to explore in the video. Again, as we did not understand the language, we had no idea of the content of his narrative at the time. However, we found his prolific response and relaxed attitude to us and the camera encouraging. Mashaile also invited us to come and stay with him at his post and said he would slaughter a sheep for us.

Screening prior to second group discussion

Subjects Speak Out

The second group screening and discussion in another valley took this interactive process a step further. Many of the herders in this group had participated in the first group discussion and it was their second viewing of the video. In this case Remaketse opened discussion by asking: "Do you have any comments on what you have seen in the film?" One herder, Chere (who had arrived at the first group discussion but had been unable to pick up on the discussion and subsequently left) emerged as the chief protagonist in this group. The transcript (Appendix 3) shows him questioning the opinion of the other herders and asking them to explain themselves and justify their opinions.

When herder (1) answers "We don't have any comments", another herder (2) questions this: "We don't have any comments?"

H1: Yes
H2: Is it because you understood what was being said?
H1: Yes
H2: What did they say to start with, maybe you will make us agree with what we do not know
H1: No, I do not make you agree with what you do not understand
H2: What did you understand from it?
H1: I understood what they said
Chere: What did they say, we want to hear from you
H1: I was still (not?) there. I do not have to answer for those people who might be making mistakes.
H2: Did you not understand what they were talking about?
C: I agree with what people said that the animals must graze on the grazing lands in a good way, truly.
H2: Yes, but did you hear that they can graze but we should be aware of the quality of grazing and whether the number of posts should be increased. So what can you say about that point?
C: The number of posts will increase
H2: It will increase? Yes, being aware of the quality of grazing...Yes..that will satisfy the animals.
C: The animals, because the Basotho nation is growing, so they will increase and the number of posts will increase?
H3: Where will they graze?
C: They will graze, in this matter the Basotho must limit their animals.

To this highly contentious statement everyone responds at once. Following on from this the discussion moved beyond individual views to conflict (on how and at what number to limit herd size), and later resolution

40

within the group on the crucial issues of herd numbers and who was entitled to establish a cattle post. This discussion lasted for over an hour and was again followed by the herders volunteering to sing for us. They also requested that we take individual photographic portraits of them, and most of them threw off their blankets (leaving them bare chested) and struck impressive poses.

Recording group discussion in Jareteng

We also recorded Chere explaining the use of a certain plant to treat animals. This was one of the few occasions where we needed to det-up and re-shoot a sequence, as he had pulled the plant from the ground very quickly and I had missed the action. However, it was necessary to re-shoot in order to record the plant in the ground, Chere removing it, demonstrating how the sap was squeezed out of the leaf and explaining what it was used for.

A later screening and discussion with a group of younger herders revealed a different set of concerns for the teenagers:

Herder: On what has been talked about I comment on herders' education. I will be very happy to be helped with education and a road must be built up here. It is rumoured that a road is to be built from Mokhotlong to here and from Natal. I can be very happy but other things like improving grazelands and things like that I am not clear because I never attended any gathering.

R: The first time you saw all the cameras and equipment here how did you take it?

H: Truly they frightened me because I first saw them from the white man. I first saw them at Sani taking photographs and shooting but I couldn't know what would happen, why they were doing that

R: So when we showed the video how did you take it after that?

H: It became clear to me because I saw some of the people I know

R: So will you encourage other people in future not to be frightened and to be free to give of their opinions?

H: Yes.

The view of another herder.

Mpiti: From what I have seen in the movie I don't criticise anything. I find it good to appear on the screen for far people to see how I live and my problems.

Mpiti was relating not only his response to the film of other herders but the connection that as we had videoed him that morning he would too end up in a 'movie'. In fact, he had become very animated for the camera and at one point threw off his blanket and flexed his muscles while sitting astride a ram. Tim suggested I stop filming so as to not encourage any further 'showing-off'.

Sheep As Subjects

The shoot with Mpiti also revealed a number of interesting insights relating to the problems inherent in reconstructing events. While we were camped at his post there was an icy wind blowing and we were huddled in his hut trying to keep warm. Mpiti was outside in a pair of ragged shorts with a blanket slung loosely around him (standard herder dress) seemingly oblivious to the freezing cold. He had a bowl of salt and was making a clicking sound with his tongue. One by one the sheep started coming up to him to eat from the bowl. I decided to film this and proceeded to fetch the camera and tripod and set it up a few metres away from him. However, all this activity frightened off the sheep, and they now stood some distance off staring at me and refused to respond to Mpiti's repeated calls. After leaving the camera standing there for some time they slowly returned. By the time I eventually recorded some of this, they were still jittery and the intimacy between herder and flock I had witnessed had been lost in my intervention. A similar thing occurred with counting the sheep. I later saw Mpiti leaning next to the kraal allowing one sheep at a time to emerge and counting the off with his hand in a casual and practised manner. I quickly collected the camera and rushed over only to see the last sheep disappear. Mpiti realised I had wanted to film this and herded them all back inside, which I recorded. But the recording of him counting the sheep had again lost spontaneity as his actions were exaggerated and the sheep hesitant to emerge.

Sheep turned out to be the most difficult subjects to engage. They definitely displayed acute camera awareness and marked change in behaviour. We had considered a shot of a herder bringing in the sheep at the end of the day as an essential image as it was so central to their daily routine. However, this was easier thought than done. The sheep are trained to follow a certain grazing routine and leave and return to the kraal by themselves at specific times. Unfortunately it turned out this time was just after the sun had dipped behind the mountains and by the time they were all encouraged into the kraal by the herder the light was usually murky. As a result we had to reconstruct this event, and had selected Mashaile to do it, to tie in with his extended dialogue. Again the sheep were very reluctant (and confused) to find themselves suddenly being driven home at an unusual hour, and this 'action' sequence is very different from the usually languid and mellow close of day.

The 'Ideal' Subject

Mashaile Kapa is an 'ideal' herder. At 23-years-old he has built up his own herd of 37 sheep, is busy building his own post, and has set himself a goal of 70 stock in three years time. He is an example of the aspirations of all young herders to become their own stock and cattlepost owners. We arrived at his cattlepost to a hot meal of grilled mutton which was most welcome, though we were disappointed that we had missed another opportunity to record a sheep being slaughtered. We had been considering the option of a central character (or 'Representative Individual' à la Flaherty) to substitute for a narrator as a way of creating continuity in the video, and thought Mashaile seemed suitable. He appeared relaxed in the presence of the camera and enthusiastic to contribute to the video. We later selected the first part of his dialogue as the beginning of the video (after a reflexive introduction) due to its poetic and moving feel:

"I am 23 years old. I want to marry when I am 27 if God answers my wishes, because that is natural. I wish he helps me to have worked by the time I marry because here I am in a wilderness, having no female company (having left girl's saliva). Here it is cold, its desolate where Christ was born. God has protected us up here from any enemies. This wilderness wants a person who renounces himself. Someone who enjoys the sweetness of life will not stay here."

That evening we recorded Mashaile, an old man and a young boy preparing and sharing supper inside his hut. This is a very intimate and revealing sequence which begins with Steve saying "From now on no English is spoken...". Mashaile had a tatty paperback with a picture of a Trojan horse which he showed to the other herders and they found it amusing. We could see that he treasured it as he carefully replaced it on a rock ledge. I immediately saw this 'happening' as a link into the education issues, illustrating the herders striving for knowledge, but only able to look at the pictures. He also showed us his three worn photographs which Tim had taken and given to him on previous trips. Tim spoke to the old man about livestock and grazing issues. This prompted Mashaile to ask the old man about the history of the cattleposts in the valley. The 'naturalness' of this sequence was the result of both Tim's long-standing friendship with Mashaile and the relationship we (as crew) had built up with him. He had also become 'at ease' and almost unaware of the camera's presence.

Supper at Mashaile's

Village Views

We spent the next night at the village of Draaihoek en route back to Mokhotlong. Tim wanted to buy another horse (which as it turns out it didn't even belong to the man trying to sell it to us). This was a long and protracted process at the end of which we were presented with a sheep (which later 'starred' in our reconstruction of a slaughter). We used the time in the village to interview a cattlepost owner about livestock, grazing, range management, and stock tax. We also recorded a cattle breeder. This we set up inside a 'kraal', to provide visual variety and to link his dialogue with the subject matter.

On our return to Mokhotlong we visited the sheep shearing sheds and recorded the shearing and sorting of wool. We attempted to speak to some of the shearers but the sound quality was poor. Tim located the person in charge and we interviewed him outside with the shed in the background. Tim was very pleased with this interview as he felt the man had explained the market economy of Lesotho and the impact of the global wool market (even referring to the Iraqi war) in easily understood terms.

Evaluation Of The Second Trip And Video Screenings

We were very encouraged by the results of this trip. We had made significant advances in our interaction with herders and had also recorded a great deal of material (over seven hours). The demonstration video had made a big difference. We had been able to communicate to herders about film generally and the video project specifically, as well as raise issues (though the presentation of the views of other herders) which had enabled them to voice their own opinions and to determine what they saw as important. These discussions had illustrated the benefits of group

Recording a group discussion

action in raising problems, discussing them, revealing individual concerns and ultimately reaching consensus on issues.

Apart from our 'reflexive' recording of this process most of the footage was predominantly the views of the herders. The group discussions had also significantly altered the power relations between 'us' and 'them' and resulted in a far more 'democratic' interaction. The herders had realised the ability of video to communicate their concerns to a wider audience and the 'power' this gave their views. Though they were talking to us, it is also the Lesotho government and range management officials they are addressing through the camera. The video screenings and group discussions that followed stimulated the articulation of herders frustrations and created a forum for herders to both address their grievances to the authorities, and to resolve differences in opinion between them. This process also revealed a transformation of traditional power relations between elders and children.

In the group discussion including Chere, a young herder speaks out against the opinions of the older herders and is allowed to debate his point. In this sense the presence of a camera also has the potential to develop positive relations of interaction. As the herders realised their ability to communicate through the camera they used the opportunity to project their 'voice' to those in authority.

Developing The Rough Script

Remaketse returned to Durban with us in order to transcribe the material we had recorded. This was the producers' first direct contact with content and clear understanding of the herders' views. We had been against the idea of using a narrator due to the inevitable position of dominance this 'voice of authority' takes on. We were now faced with the problem of how to create continuity and context without narration. On the strength of the material we opted for the indirect mode of address common to *cinéma verité*. We selected dialogue from the interviews and group discussions on the basis of presenting a wide range of views and to highlight herders concerns (Appendix 3). These were structured so as to try and create continuity and cover all the issues that had emerged, i. e. education, working conditions, lifestyles, livestock management, and environmental concerns. This was done primarily on paper between Steve, Tim and myself, and no consideration was given to specific shot selection and visual overlays.

What did emerge was that the content reflected a video not only ON herders but FOR herders, as they talk for themselves and agitate for changes to their living and working conditions. They revealed an awareness of the problems threatening their livelihood and a sense of urgency to find solutions to the predicament of increasing stock numbers and dwindling natural resources. Their 'voice' emerges as an appeal to be heard by authority and to be given a say in determining their future.

We were now one step closer to a product and returned to the question of audience. As the video was now mostly in Sesotho we decided to use subtitles to translate dialogue into English to enable the video to reach a wider audience. We also drew up a shot list of links and contextualising interviews for the next trip.

Trip 3 (Winter): Consolidation/Integration

To overcome the problems of context and continuity which emerged following our decision not to use a narrator we planned to record a number of linking sequences in the field to weave into our edited script. The resulting shot list looked like this:

Tim on the history of the project (Herders context)
Steve and Chuck on progression of project, methods, use demo film.
Remaketse on herding experience
Interviews in village on why people keep livestock
Tim on political and economic context livestock economy
Tim on history of cattleposts and wool industry
Remaketse on why went to the mines and why returned.
Remaketse on free time of herders
Tim on theft, natural disasters
Tim on diseases facing livestock
Tim on grazing management
Craig on conservation problems and deteriorating grasslands
Craig on scientific view of grasslands
Various questions for future policy.

We were now effectively adding our 'voice' in addition to our presence in the video, but we felt it necessary to balance the languages (for English audiences) and to relate herder concerns to a broader context.

Trip 3: Consolidation And Integration

We were accompanied on the winter trip (July 1991) by ecologist Craig Morris, his wife Anita, and a photographer from the University of Durban-Westville, Fiona Clyde. This much larger group and the adverse winter conditions (freezing cold, short days) once again hampered our plans and progress. We were delayed in Mapholaneng arranging extra horses and donkeys. We used the time to interview a local herbalist on the healing properties of plants and recorded Tim talking about the importance of livestock in Lesotho and the role of cattle in village life.

The Best Laid Plans...

Once we had finally started on the journey to the winter cattleposts the most telling setback was when Remaketse fell ill (with what turned out to be tonsillitis) and was unable speak, let alone conduct interviews. This revealed our reliance on him for communication, and the crucial role he played in our interaction with herders. We were now unable to effectively hold discussions with herders. However, we pressed on to Mashaile's cattlepost (in the 'summer' area) hoping to use him for some of the links. Unfortunately, he had gone 'down' to his village. Our presence at the post once again attracted a crowd of herders who asked to see a 'filim'. We used the same demonstration video we had shown on the second trip, and they seemed disappointed that it had not included the footage of them we had recorded on the second trip. Following this screening we only spoke briefly to the herder who was standing in for Mashaile.

We decided to head for the 'winter' posts where the majority of herders had moved to. En route one of our pack horses went lame. This made up our minds to return to our transit base at Mateanong while Tim and Fiona went on to the 'winter' posts. Without both Remaketse and Tim (and the ability to speak Sesotho) we reverted back to standard documentary techniques, filming village life and setting up and conducting interviews in English. We had recorded links with Tim and Craig, and located a range management official, Frances Ntale, who we interviewed (in English) to a set of formulated questions. 'What is the Range Management Project?, Why a need for it? How was it developed? Explain the need for cattleposts?, What about disease and theft, stock numbers and control?'. This provided us with many of the links we had originally allocated to Tim. He also told about a 'workshop' for herders they were holding the following month (this was videoed by Tim and Remaketse).

Once Remaketse had regained his voice we interviewed a Village Range Supervisor in Sesotho on how range management implemented on a village level. We also managed to locate Mashaile at his village and spoke to him and his employer. Unfortunately he was unable to elaborate on his ambitions in the presence of his employer.

As most of the cattle return to the villages in winter it turned out that through force of circumstance we were in the right place at the right time. We were able to record the role of cattle in village life which would help to portray the importance of livestock in the rural areas.

Evaluation: Trip 3

While we were disappointed with what we had been able to achieve on this trip, we felt that we already had enough material for the video and were happy to fill-in and develop some of the areas examined. In this sense, through both design and circumstance, we had shifted the focus of this trip from process back to product. In addition we had reverted back to more conventional documentary production techniques by working to a pre-determined schedule and selecting the content we needed to fit into our draft editing script.

Project Overview

In order to draw out the strands of reflection in the preceding description I will now examine the emergent relationships within the whole project through the use of the: (INTENTION) - Anthropologist - Producer - Process - Subjects - Audience - (PURPOSE) framework (Tomaselli et al., 1986, p. 37).

Intention

The prime intention of facilitating herder self-expression and enabling the articulation of their issues and concerns through creating dialogue met with varying degrees of success on each of the field trips (an evaluation of whether we achieved 'empowerment' of the subject-community will be examined in the following theoretical analysis of our use of 'community video' method). Our ability to realise our intentions was directly related to practical problems we encountered on location and the strategies we adopted to overcome language and cultural barriers. Our limited success with engaging herders (on the first trip) through direct interaction and the use of interview techniques, led us to the more indirect intervention of the demonstration video, which as a means, justified the end, in that it achieved the stimulation of herder opinions and triggered discussion.

Our intention to document the production process and relations of interaction through the adoption of a reflexive method was easier to achieve. In this component we were both producers and subjects and were able to structure this content through both deliberate self-reflection and incidental incorporation of our presence into the filming process.

Our pre-conception of the intended product evolved in the production process. While we essentially controlled the form of the representation (video production) and had defined (and implemented) the field of study (Herder lifestyle) the herders themselves gained greater input to and determination of the content. As we achieved a 'cross-cultural communication' of our intentions and they established their participation in the production they were able to articulate their own concerns, raise and debate issues, and define them in their own terms.

What did emerge was also a contradiction between purpose and practice. While our intentions informed our decisions in the field, often we were forced to adapt to practical circumstances. This was apparent on the first trip when the intimidating impact of the crew and equipment conflicted with our intention to draw out herders' views. On the third trip, our communication breakdown through the loss of Remaketse's participation, left us to fall back on filming 'happenings' and finding English interviewees. There was therefore no linear development of progressively achieving our objectives, but rather fluctuations where some recording situations conformed to our interactive intentions while others were unsuccessful.

Anthropologist

Tim had a key role to play in the project, both through his wealth of experience in the region as an anthropologist, and his position as instigator and organiser of the video production. In this sense it is necessary to distinguish between the Producer-Director functions of a production, with Tim taking on the conventional role of Producer, while Steve and myself were responsible for the technical and aesthetic considerations of a director.

Initially our production imperatives were dictated by Tim's research objectives. This entailed visiting as many cattleposts and interviewing as many herders as possible. This soon created tensions, with us questioning the necessity and value of unloading and setting up the equipment to record every interaction with every herder we met. Tim was also aware that the anthropological methods of 'participant observation' and 'immersion in the community' were significantly distorted by the presence of a the cameras and crew, and was concerned about introducing the filming aspect in a 'sensitive' way. To this end his ability to speak Sesotho and the fact he was known by many herders was a great help. He was also instrumental in formulating the questions to ask herders and through his experience of making his previous two videos had a clear idea of what he wanted to incorporate (and avoid) in the video. He was therefore well qualified to infuse the process with an 'ethnographic understanding' of the herders situation within the broader context of the livestock economy and range management issues.

Producers

We were guided as much by working against dominant documentary conventions (eg. avoiding an imposed process and structured filming) as we were working to any specific guidelines. However, our realisation that a product-centric approach dominates people, led us to draw on our respective experience of democratic production process at community organisation level, and focus on developing an interactive and participatory process.

The reflexive use of the second camera was my priority, while Steve was primarily concerned with the technical quality of the main production. He insisted on taking the U-matic equipment (separate camera and VCR, bulky tapes) on the last two trips despite the additional load and immobility in the field. Video production inevitably requires making decisions when recording and this did create tensions between us when deciding on how to shoot something. These were usually resolved by, "well if that's how you want to do it. DO IT!".

We were also concerned with integrity and avoided staging events for camera or directing response to camera - although we were guilty of these to an extent. Our inability to understand Sesotho alienated us from content and as a result we became largely technical functionaries of our process. In this role we controlled form through the selection shots, when to start, "OK it's rolling you can begin", and when to stop, "Hold it, the tape's finished". This is the area where internalised production practices and creative considerations begin to impact upon process. We were aware that the techniques of camera operation influence visual impact, and felt the concern with the aesthetics of framing was counteracted by our reflexive approach which included the microphone, interviewer, and ourselves in the framed picture.

Directors are ultimately responsible for the selection and ordering of content to visual conventions. We had total control over the form and presentation of the demonstration video, and had influenced the content of the video through the shot list of links for the third trip. The draft editing script had evolved out of consultation between us and was constantly being revised. Editing also requires decisions on which visual material to overlay on which interviews and it is here that many distortions can take place.

We had consciously attempted to defuse power relations between us and our subjects through enabling interaction by playing back recorded material and by revealing our intentions and methods. We were also concerned with exposing the production process though reflexive practice and establishing our ethnographic presence as part of the subject matter.

Process

We started out without any strict shooting schedule and only a rough outline to areas to be covered and visuals needed. Our commitment to engaging and enabling herder participation in the project led us from: "We'd like to speak to you about", to "We'd like you to speak to us about", to "We'd like to show you a film", as means of generating response and developing interaction. While we initially formulated questions, and mostly initiated contact, we ultimately enabled our subjects to express themselves to camera.

This was initially through the use of video playback, which only had limited success compared with the demonstration video screenings. Through screening the video we were able to communicate an understanding of video in general and the specific nature our project. This helped to overcome the conventional divide between crew and subjects and promoted a collaborative examination of issues. The group discussions created a forum for the herders to raise and articulate issues on their own terms and the camera's presence stimulated (rather than intimidated) subjects to voice their opinions.

We realised that the camera is not a neutral object and that it impacts on and changes the nature of a situation, and the way it is introduced determines whether it interferes in the situation or whether it allows subjects to reveal and express themselves. Our experience found that interpersonal interaction also had a large part to play and that it was necessary to establish a personal relationship with subjects, and to introduce the function of the equipment, in order to overcome its intimidating effect. Technical considerations also impact on interaction as the setting up of equipment draws attention to the crew and creates a sense of expectancy that needs to be defused.

Remaketse played a leading role in the process as he was the only one able to fluently communicate with the subjects. As the interviewer he often directed interaction and was invaluable in establishing a rapport with subjects. His presence in the crew and familiarity with the equipment also contributed to our acceptance by the subjects.

As the operator of the 'reflexive camera' I sometimes found myself outside the primary relations of crew and subjects and setting up another set of relations observing the observers observe. As we developed this approach we came to regard the second camera as a 'participant observer' and became less self-conscious as we got used to its presence. Combined with the integrated nature of our field work, this made the process a learning experience for all the participants as it stimulated self-evaluation and debate around the way we formulated questions, our relations of interaction with the herders, and the synthesis of ideas into video representation.

The physical conditions of working in the field also influenced the process. Gerald Millerson sums up the nature of these difficulties,

> ... away from the studio, the opportunities for coverage and treatment are invariably limited. The considerable areas and distances often involved at remotes, the limitations of facilities and the environmental problems all influence production potentials. Lightweight cameras provide mobility, but various inherent problems (local acoustics, extraneous noise, weather, light variations, continuity, etc.) must affect treatment. (Millerson, 1979, p. 276)

This was very much the case with our own experience, and decisions regarding the quality of material will have to be made during editing. However, we were primarily concerned with process and content, and though frustrated by the often adverse conditions, we felt the rough form reflected the nature of the video and context in which it was made. By adopting this approach the nature of the process becomes an integral part of the product .

Subjects

Our encounters with the herders and their response to us was partly related to the ratio of the number of crew to the number of herders. On the first trip we often outnumbered our subjects and this intrusion initially effected their behaviour and stifled response. This was also due to the formal nature of the interview situation. The screenings of the demon-stration video created a totally different form of interaction. The large groups brought together young and old, and a cross section of opinions. They responded both to the herders they had seen on the video and to the views of one another.

These interactions also revealed a pleasure and willingness by herders to demonstrate their talents and abilities for the camera once they had realised who we were and what we were doing. While we were pri-marily interested in their views, they would draw our attention to their musical talents and other skills, such as spinning wool, knitting woollen caps and stick fighting. This evolved through a process of 'cross-cultural communication', as we managed to explain our presence and the project, so the herders were able to realise and determine their contribution to the video. In this way the group encounters defused the power relations between us and created a collective forum for the herders to express themselves and debate issues.

Loi

We were also able to develop individual relationships with herders that overcame the separation between the observers and the observed. For example, recording the intimacy of sharing dinner with Mashaile in his hut was only possible through his invitation and willing participation.

The reflexive footage also established the crew as subjects. While this reveals our presence to the audience there is also a danger that we can assume a position of prominence above the main subject of herder lifestyles and concerns and this needs to be avoided.

Audience
The present conception of the video aims at reaching a variety of different audiences. The evolution from a video about herders to a video *for* herders has positioned it as an intervention advocating on their behalf to the authorities in Lesotho. We also plan to screen it in Lesotho for the herders and in rural villages.

The raw footage provides valuable source data for academic use and it has already been used in this context. The reflexive footage reveals our video production methods and provides material for further analysis and discussion. A final product emerging out of the process of further interaction and input from herders would hopefully reach a general

From screening to group of herders in Jareteng

audience. The idea is to subtitle the completed video from Sotho to English and enable it to reach an English-reading audience.

In terms of form and technical quality it is unlikely to meet broadcast standards. We would hope it will be distributed to libraries and reach students and ethnographic film audiences.

Towards A Theoretical Understanding

Ethnographic film as an area of study has been incorporated into the broader field of Visual Anthropology, reflecting the shift in focus from product to process-based methodologies as well as the increased use of video as a more immediate and accessible visual medium. However, the divide between theory and practice, or more precisely between method and theorising practice remains. Our work in Lesotho incorporated a number of different, and even contradictory, production practices, which when isolated, or emphasised, could be located within various frameworks.

If we choose to focus on our subjects, their cultural context, and our reflexive approach, the project could conform to the broad categories of ethnographic film product and process. We have ended up with a form that could also fit into the 'narrated-documentary informed by ethnographic understanding and revealing production methods'-model of ethnographic film. Instead we have a hybrid that uses the indirect address of *cinéma verité* within a narrative structure more akin to documentary. Our organisation and presentation of content evolved out of our emphasis on process above product, and specifically our adaption of 'participatory' or 'community video' methods.

Community Video Debates

In a joint paper with Costas Criticos, the Director of the Media Resource Centre at the University of Natal in Durban, Tim Quinlan theorises the herders video within the 'Community Video'- model. Entitled *Putting Education and Anthropology to work: Community Video and Ethnographic Documentation in South Africa* (1991), the article focuses on the potential of community video for the 'collective' social construction of knowledge.

> The emphasis of community video on full participation by 'subjects' of a film and on participant reflection on issues addressed in a film indicate that it can be a powerful means of political, cultural and scientific expression. (1991, p. 2)

Criticos's 'educational perspective' is 'derived from principles of Participatory Research and critical pedagogy' (Ibid, p. 5) and based on Freire's related theories of 'cultural action' and 'dialogic' education, 'in which learning is a collaborative task which builds on the skills and experience of both learner and teacher' (Ibid, p. 3). Criticos thereby frames community video as an emancipatory tool with the educational potential to achieve praxis ('... if participants make the linkage between theory and practice' (Ibid, p. 4)) through its '... collaborative and dialogic nature' (Ibid, p. 3). He examines this proposition in relation to the video project *Hanging up the nets*, which he produced in collaboration with the Durban Bay Fishing community.

Quinlan develops this line of thought from an 'anthropological perspective' and states that community video

> ... promotes the participants' critical awareness of what they are doing, of the world around them, and it reveals opportunities for constructive community and individual intervention in that world. The community video project stimulates amongst participants a collective construction of knowledge and meaning about the world. (Ibid, p. 11)

Quinlan's focus is on community video as a '... powerful research instrument' as it '... brings into the open the process of constructing knowledge, and offers immediate opportunities for reflection and debate with informants on social issues' (Ibid, p. 12). He also acknowledges that, '... the community video approach presumes knowledge of, if not familiarity with video', and that this lack of understanding amongst the herders '... proved a limitation to discussion of the issues to be addressed in the film' (Ibid, p. 14). Quinlan describes how our use of the demonstration video addressed this problem and argues that the resultant group discussions '... initiated the process of creating a 'community' amongst herders who expressed interest in participating in the project' (Ibid, p. 15).

This idea of a 'community in media' is defined by Criticos as:

> Community in media means that the community, ie. a collective community of common struggle, has collective and democratic engagement in the contents, production and distribution of community media [and] ...explores the development of collective production methods and collective creativity'. (Tomaselli, 1989, p. 12)

This attempt to theorise 'community' creates a number of problems in the context of the *Lesotho Herders Video Project*. We were not dealing with an established community but rather a disparate group which shares a common livelihood, common conditions of existence, concerns, and (a large) geographic proximity. However, Tim argues that we constituted 'a community' through the 'collective and democratic engagement' in articulating the content of the video and the process of exposing areas of 'common struggle'. Further we (the crew) make up part of that community as reflected in the video.

The problem here is that while the project defines the 'community' in terms of 'common struggle' (by both producers and subjects), the power of the herders, in this case, to express their 'own' opinions, is out-weighed by the producers' control over the representation of herder concerns. In practice the subject-community in both the projects examined by Quinlan and Criticos have only limited (if any) participation in the production methods. However, the real strength of these projects is their to mobilise the subject-community and enable them to claim 'ownership' of the content.

In a highly theorised response to Criticos and Quinlan's paper, Roger Deacon (1992) identifies that their reflections are based in critical theory's belief in the potential for individuals to reach 'enlightenment' and 'empowerment' through critical reflection, and thereby liberate themselves from relations of dominance and change the world.

Deacon argues that through the community video practices adopted by Criticos and Quinlan this potential 'end' is negated by the contradiction within the 'means' of constituting, controlling and implementing projects,

> CV as such is necessarily constituted in advance by various 'assumptions' (knowledge) and 'interference' (power) which unavoidably condition both the process and the product of the project ...It is relatively insignificant whether these are 'democratic' as apposed to 'autocratic' interferences, or whether researchers do or do not impose their views; rather what is important is how power-knowledge, taking any or all of these forms, operates through the vehicles of the researchers, their subjects and the research process itself. (1992, p. 17)

However, Deacon acknowledges that '... though the projects as critical theories have failed to transform their respective communities, the

61

projects in themselves produced changes and benefits for both communities and researchers' (Ibid, p. 11). As the researchers become their own subjects (of reflection and analysis), ultimately only they benefit from critical reflection upon and decision making about their practices.

Deacon points out the absence of herder participation in decision-making and the technical production processes. He identifies the paradox within this model as the subject-communities 'lack the theoretical tools necessary to reflect on and transform practice supposedly democratically involved in' (Ibid:12) and therefore the necessity to 'transform' subjects in advance through the educational intervention of the demonstration video. As a result 'attempts to encourage such self-emancipation by stressing participation and reflexivity tended to exacerbate (this) contradiction by over-emphasising practice at the expense of critique' (Ibid, p. 12).

While Deacon identifies a number of key problems with theorising the community video method, the strength of his argument has more to do with the contradictions within the 'praxis' of these specific projects than a total dismissal of a community video method. While both projects are motivated by the best of intentions the focus on democratic practice disguises the degree of intervention (power) of the researchers. As Tomaselli points out '... academics ... tend to create a discourse about a community which has more to do with their own positions in society than with actual situations on the ground' (1989, p. 12). This applies as much to Deacon's response as to the researchers' theorising of their respective projects. The danger is that researchers subscribing to 'participatory' methods may claim 'democratic practice' to lend credibility to the project and findings, while this 'participation' often only involves subject approval and consent within a defined area of debate or study (knowledge).

Agitating For Advocacy

In the arena of academic discourse community video methods are easy to expose, problematic to implement, and the results difficult to justify. However, we need to resolve the contradictions rather than discredit the methods and intent. The fact that community video is a 'process' highlights its emergent nature. These are just the first steps. If we accept the need to actively engage communities and develop the skills of the disadvantaged before 'empowerment' can even begin, we need to transcend academia and start practising what we preach. While community video method creates the space for community participation and aims to facilitate the transfer of skills, we need to focus on developing processes and production methods that achieve these goals. It is only through an on-going process that problems can be overcome. The potential cannot be denied.

> There is indeed no other medium like video which offers ordinary people so much choice and therefore freedom, so much creativity and therefore self assertion and growth, and so much collective knowledge and experience and therefore learning. ... In Chile, for example, an alternative video network has been built up which amounts to a formidable political, social and cultural force. The learning and conscientisation process now takes place between groups which, without VCR's, could not easily be in contact with each other. (Traber and Lee, 1989, p. 1)

Many other projects throughout the Third World have realised these claims and shown the ability of video to mobilise and empower communities. The experience of the *Popular Video Project* which works with grassroots communities in Brazil found:

> ... video's collective experience considerably different from watching TV at home. The videos prompt people to discuss local problems and possible solutions. Examples of what was done in other places gives new ideas and proof that it is possible for them to take the situation into their own hands. (Ceccon, 1989, p. 31)

In the same way the *Lesotho Herder Video Project* evolves from a video *about* herders to a video *of* and *for* herders. Relating this back to Deacon's argument, while he makes an important point on how power-knowledge operates through the vehicles of the researchers, his conclusion that ultimately only the researchers benefit from critical reflection on and decision-making about their practices is questionable when related to the recorded group discussions amongst herders. The content of these discussions (Appendix 3) demonstrates that the subjects *are* critically evaluating conservation and livestock problems and reflecting on how these issues affect their livelihoods. We don't speak for them, they speak for themselves, but we do speak with them, and although their views are integrated into 'our' form, their voice gains precedence and meaning is negotiated through collaboration. 'They' emerge to claim the content as their 'own' and articulate issues on their own terms.

By defining the researchers, subjects and the process as 'vehicles' for 'power-knowledge', Deacon denies the potential of the individuals and the process to actively re-define power relations and to transcend 'assumptions'.

> In Columbia, individuals trained in anthropology and film make movies that are useful outside the classrooms. Some anthropologists have contributed their knowledge to films made with the collaboration of the base communities and with individuals trained in film. There is an effort in these cases to TRANSCEND ACADEMIA by broadening its goals and modifying the dehumanized norm of the observer and the observed. When there is active participation of individuals in both research and film, object becomes subject and the product is useful in science-action. In many instances, the, ethnographic films have functioned as communication tools among local communities, between these and government policy circles, and even among guerilla formations. (De Brigard, 1983, p. 320)

A broader framework for evaluating whether or not the Lesotho project achieves its 'community video' objectives in practice (rather than in theory) is to rate it in terms of Tomaselli's characteristics of community video (Table of Differences: pages 7-8). In the categories of 'Communication/Knowledge/Coding/Production' the Lesotho project is consistent with community video practices. It is in the area of 'Questions of Democracy/Distribution/Power, Empowerment' that the line is not so clearly defined, although the project still conforms with the community video intent, rather than conventional practices.

Participation A Key To Praxis?
It would seem then that the major difficulty is with the question of how participatory a community video project is. Is it enough to redefine the production process to provide a 'voice' for subject communities? At what point is 'empowerment' achieved? On the one hand the method-ologies tried by Worth provide only technical and organisational assis-

tance and leave the producer-trainees to define their own subjects and determine their own construction of meaning.

On the other hand, Edmund Carpenter's experiments with putting the camera in the hand of the other while working with villagers in New Guinea conclude:

> The media permit little experimentation and only a person of enormous power and sophistication is capable of escaping their binding power. A very naive person may stumble across some interesting technique,...the trend is otherwise. (quoted by Anderson, 1985, p. 33)

In the case of the *Lesotho Herders Video Project* it has thus far not been practical to enable technical control due to time and practical constraints and this has led to questions on how to structure and select the transfer of technical skills, and even doubts, 'Is this necessary in this context?'.

The experience of equivalent projects elsewhere in the world have shown that medium term 'collaborative' processes to transfer skills should aim at developing into long term 'empowerment' through which the potential for 'emancipation' is achievable. A whole new wave of 'indigenous TV' in Australia, India, and Latin America is challenging the hegemonic hold of the dominant TV codes of fantasy dressed up as reality. This self-expression is emerging from a 'real' world of hardship, suffering and oppression, and presents a voice and image of human dignity that cannot but be taken seriously - 'Video by the people for the people'. An example is the work being done in the remote Australian outback community of Ernabella:

> Our experience proved that instead of subverting traditional culture to conform with the materialist and various sensationalist concerns of 'whitefella' mass media. TV can be creatively employed by Aboriginal people to strengthen their own communicative process and foster pride in unique cultural and artistic forms. (Turner, 1986, p. 43)

The numerous attempts to realise the democratic potential of video technology are not only limited to the Third World. In Holland the *Video Bus Project* was founded by the Dutch Institute for Community Development (NIMO) to provide training in production skills to marginalised communities throughout the country. The aim was to facilitate 'affirmative access' for groups to community TV stations and production facilities (Media Development 4/1989, p. 23).

These developments reflect a global awareness of the urgent need to find alternatives to the hegemony of dominant TV products and codes. It is only through the transfer of production skills and eventual access to broadcasting alternative views will emerge and be heard.

> Only when Aboriginal people control the production can a genuinely Aboriginal TV product emerge. A black face on the screen might look good (and will appease some vocal critics) but the real power lies on the other side of the camera. It is the producers, directors and the financial managers who are really in control. (Central Australian Aboriginal Media Association Manifesto)

It is important that we do not limit our attention solely to the process, as 'new' approaches to form and product also need to be considered. The deliberate manipulations and distortions of Trinh T. Minh-ha, blend observation and reflection in poetic narrative form, creating a dualism that challenges interpretation and aims to, '...convey a multiplicity of readings, much of the film should be that which I do not fully control'. Her work reflects a refusal to define the 'other' as 'object of study' and an attempt extinguish all forms of identity and subjectivity. An example of narrative from her film *Reassemblage*:

> *Scarcely 20 years were enough to make two billion people define themselves as underdeveloped*
>
> *I do not intend to speak about*
> *Just speak nearby*
>
> *The Casamance*
> *Sun and palms*
> *the part of Senegal where tourist settlements flourish*
>
> *A film about what? my friends ask*
> *A film about Senegal; but what in Senegal?*
>
> *...Reality is delicate*

My irreality and imagination are otherwise dull
the habit of imposing meaning to every sign

She kept it in diverse places
at the end of the stick she used to dig the ground with for example.

Conclusion

The *Lesotho Herders Video Project* is still very much 'in process'. Our respective reflections on the achievements and limitations of the project have led to the realisation that we need to take the process a step further and facilitate greater participation by the herders in the final form of the video. To this end we are planning to complete a rough edit of the video which we will take back to the herders for comment and as a stimulus for further discussion. In this way we hope to build on the relationships we have already established and to enable a greater degree of herder determination in the final product.

What Achieved - For Whom

All of the participants have gained new knowledge and insights through the interactive process of the video production.

The skills and experience gained by Remaketse led to further formal technical training and participation in a documentary production workshop in Durban. He is now working on radio and video marketing programmes for a para-statal company in Lesotho which supplies water and electricity.

The herders have gained 'a voice', which will enable them to agitate for changes in their living and working conditions and 'empowers' them to influence policy-makers. Their involvement in the process of making the video also led to an examination of, and reflection on, issues that concern them. This resulted in the resolution of differences and the realisation of common concerns.

The researchers have gained an invaluable source of information which can be used in various forms; for instruction of students, to stimulate debate within academic circles, and as a complement to their research findings. They have also been able to expand their research skills, as the use of a visual medium has led them to evaluate and develop their methodology.

Encouraged by the results of this project Tim Quinlan is now involved in a regional environmental research project which will incorporate the use of 'community video' to assist researchers to refine their foci and to stimulate community organisation to resolve problems of environmental degradation.

For video producers the reflexive footage enables them to self-consciously examine their production methods and attitudes. This is a valuable learning experience which will inform their attempts to challenge conventional documentary form and establish the basis for the emergence of alternative forms of interaction and representation.

In the same way the debates raised by visual anthropology and the question of authorship and the representation of subjects have contributed to the emergence of a 'new anthropology' that moves from 'objective' analytical methods to a more dynamic interactive process. As Geertz points out the

> The new role of anthropology is to help improve communication across different societal lines: ethnicity, class, gender, language, race ... [by enhancing] cross-cultural communication ... [in order] ... to enlarge the possibility of intelligible discourse between people quite different from one another in interest, outlook, wealth and power. (1989, p. 58)

We hope that we have gone some way toward achieving this 'cross-cultural communication' in our process, and ultimately through the final video. Our adoption of community video methods has instilled in us a sense of accountability to the herders, and, for the present, we remain the custodians of their 'voice'.

References

Anderson, P. (1985), 'The Tiakeni Report: The maker and the problem of method in documentary video production', *Critical Arts*, Vol. 4, no. 1.

Ceccon, C. S. P. (1989), 'Brazilian Centre shows that video is an Agent of Change', *Media Development*, Vol. XXXVI, no. 4.

Criticos, C. and T. Quinlan (1991), 'Putting Education and Anthropology to work: Community Video and Ethnographic Documentation in South Africa', *CVA Review*, Spring 1991.

Criticos, C. and T. Quinlan (1991), 'Community Video: Power and Process' (forthcoming in Visual Anthropology Review) .

Deacon, R. (1992), 'Community Video and Critical Pedagogy in South Africa', *Visual Sociology*, vol. 7, no. 2, pp. 39-48.

Gardner, R. (1957), 'Anthropology and Film', *Daedalus*, 86, pp. 341-52.

Geertz, C. (1989), 'Being There, Writing Here, *Dialogue*, Vol. 26 No. 8.

Heider, K. G. (1976), *Ethnographic Film*, University of Texas Press, Austin.

Hookham, J. (1991), 'We the Rhino: Ethnographic Aggies and the Representation of the Bushmen', *SATJ*, 5/1, pp. 24-33.

Millerson, G. (1979), *The Technique of Television Production*, Focal Press, U.K.

Nichols, B. (1981), *Ideology and the Image*, Indiana University Press, Bloomington.

Penley, C. and A. Ross (1985), 'Interview with Trinh T. Minh-ha', *Camera Obscura*, 13-14, pp. 87-111.

Ruby, J. (1976), 'The Image Mirrored: Reflexivity and the Documentary Film', *Journal of the University Film Association*, Vol. 29, no. 1, pp. 3-8.

SVA Review, Spring 1990.

Tomaselli, K. et al. (1986), *Myth, Race and Power*, Anthropos, Bellville.

Tomaselli, K. (1989), 'Transferring video skills to the community: the problem of power', *Media Development*, Vol. XXXVI, no. 4, pp. 11-15.

Tomaselli, K. and A. Lazerus (1989), 'Participatory Video: problems, prospects and a case study', *Group Media Journal*, VIII/1 SONOLUX W.G.

Tomaselli, K. and E. Sienaert (1989), 'Ethnographic Film/Video Production and Oral Documentation: The case of Piet Draghoender', *Kat River: The end of Hope*, Research in African Literatures, Vol. 20, No.2, University of Texas Press, Austin.

Traber, M. and P. Lee (1989), 'Video for animation and conscientisation', *Media Development*, Vol. XXXVI, no. 4.

Turner, N., 'Aboriginal TV', *Artlink*, vol. 10, nos. 1 & 2, pp. 43-48.

Williams, C. (ed.) (1980), *Realism and the Cinema*, Routledge and Kegan Paul, London.

Worth, S. and J. Adair (1972), *Through Navajo Eyes*, Indiana University Press, Bloomington.

Appendices

Appendix 1

Map locating the area of operation of LHVP

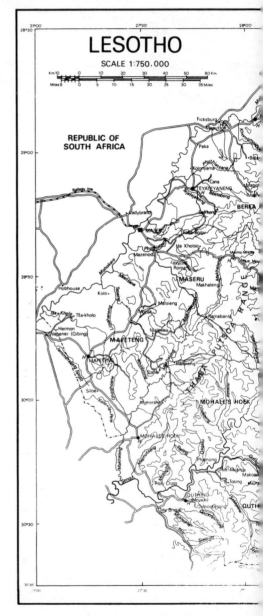

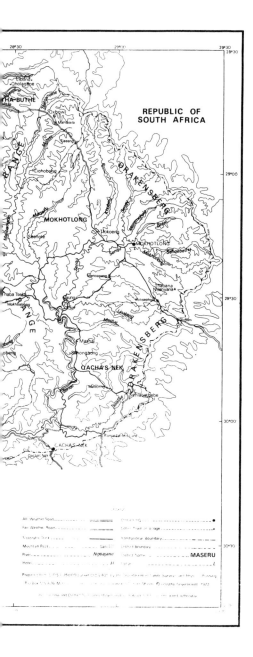

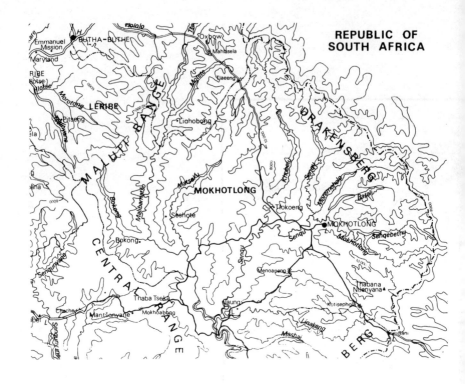

Appendices 2-8

Excerpts from transcript

Appendix 2

Mashaile Kapa's Life Story

(Transcript from footage)

1847   shot of bush he is holding, moqoboqhobo

1908   Mashaile (M): I grew up herding my father's horse. My name is Mashaile Kapa at Moseli Ntsiking. I grew up herding the horse and after that I went to school up to standard six. I had to leave school because my father was no more working and then I said to my father: "No, I'm going to work". I got hired by his uncle herding cattle at home. If I remember well it was probably eleven years I stayed with my uncle. Then I went away from my uncle to the initiation school. When I came back I went to Thabang at Khauoele's place. I worked for a year there. He paid me with a cow and I went away and got hired by Thabo Tsita at Thabang. I stayed until now. This is the fifth year being at Thabo's place. I've now 37 stock. I think in the future I want to marry having my own building (in village). I'm still young, 23 years old.

TAPE 5

0016   I am 23 years old. I want to marry when I am 27 if God answers my wishes, because that is natural (*kabelo*)

0038   I wish he helps me to have worked by the time I marry because here I am in the wilderness, having no female company. (having left girl's saliva)

0055   Here it's cold, it's desolate where Christ was born.

107   God has protected us up here from any enemies.

119   This wilderness wants a person who renounces himself (*itela*). Someone who enjoys the sweetness of life will not stay here

139   I desire that in the future my stock will not exceed seventy. When they reach seventy I exchange the ewes for hammels. I sell the hammels to get money. This thing of accumulating wealth in animals but not getting food from them ... but God has made the lamb for one to live with. But this is to argue with God and make him not give us wealth. After that a person will complain. And after losing wealth one will have little money in the bank where it is kept because it doesn't stay with a person...

242   Truly, (248) I think of that plateau. Thuathe, there I don't know when I will reach there to fetch our horses. Look at these mountains and plateaus. They are silent.

308   Now I don't know about these people who go down to the villages at the beginning of May. It is only me who stays here along with Sebokoane Kao's herder who is up at the head of the valley and Mokhotso's herder up by those cliffs. But all around here it's just me.

334   But because of God and being used to life here I don't feel bad (*bolutu*). I don't worry. I feel healthy.

350   The harshness (*sehlolo*) for a person staying up here is such that sometimes when you get home, people think that you are selfish or anti-social (*khopo*). But it's not selfishness because by the time people have gone down to the villages, one has spent about a month not speaking to anybody. Now, when you arrive there, people tend to speak to you too much and you get tired. And you think all the people are staring at you but it's not that, but it's because you have been away a long time ...it's because you have been away a long time (440 This is the time of frost NBNB black out on picture here). Last month of frost is June. May and June are the coldest months. Truly there is a lot of frost.

gap no speaking

524   Here we gather bush firewood. there is a lot of it. The bushes are all over and cover more of the land every year.

544   *Hache.*! In 1986 when I was first here in these valleys of Langalebalele and Jareteng the grass was better. The old people say that the bushes used to be just by the river and *moqhoboqhobo* used to be found the most. It was like a forest. It was like oudebas tree (*cheche*). Cheche spreads. But now it is *lelingoana* which is spreading and *sehalahala*. But when you look at the bushes there is still good grass amongst them. There's *seboku* there in the east. You find that it is still good.

644   In the west there is much *monyaphokojoe*. It is high and sheep don't graze on it because it gets into their nostrils. But when I look carefully I see that the sheep like to graze on the wetlands where we say there is nothing, but the sheep like it. The grass fills them up ... doesn't get into their nostrils and it makes them fat. Wetlands are very strong.

719   I have been to Bafali some time ago. I found many wetlands there. I found the sheep being fed such that the whole body shakes. I've never seen anything like a wetland for making small stock fat. The wetlands are really good.

804   Truly, I don't know, when I see this drought (*leballa*) I think it must snow soon and melt the drought. It is turning grey around here but the animals are still fine.

832   *Hache!* I want to go on herding. I herd and after that, after three years I will stop. I don't want to stay not doing anything. I will still come to the posts.

912   I hear stories that a person who stays at posts for a long time, when you marry you become sedentary (*ho boulela*) and forget about the animals at the posts.

80

927 Hache, they say, and I don't know, people are people, they say that you don't want anything to do with the posts (NBNB i.e. is repeating in another way previous sentence). And your wife will say with whom are you leaving me when you go.

945 After I've been asked this question, I won't feel like going to the mountains. I wish God could help me, I don't think of that. There would be dispute in the family as a result. She will have no clothes and shoes and nothing to eat. If I let the small stock go I would have nothing. But because I have stock, when I am short on cash, I can fetch one and sell it. It is bought within two days as long as it has a *babeis* (stock transfer certificate).

1039 Hache, give me some matches

1048 mutters

lights cigarette, greets someone

1120 Truly, I have got nothing more to say

1149 (Remaketse asks question) inaudible "Yes"

1159 Yes, I have already built the walls of my own post.

1205 (Remaketse asks question, inaudible)

1216 I have built only. The chiefs don't allow us to do this. I don't know I would like to talk to them...

1237 This area is prohibited to outsiders. I find it a waste of time (NB disjointed sentences)

1306 From last year, even this year, people have just been building posts without consulting the chiefs. Now you can see that line of posts, another line there...

Remaketse: Why do you want to build your own post instead of sharing?

1330 Hache! To share a post is difficult because sometimes the stock of the people sharing the post will harm each other...

R: How do the stock harm each other?

1402 Your stock will decrease by dying gradually. But when you are alone they will die at a normal rate. Like others who don't share a post.

R:

1428 Hache, a young person

R: (intervenes) No, a person of your age who owns the same number of stock as you.

M: Yes, someone like me. I encourage them. But to own a post is difficult. You need to buy food regularly. To buy food is hard because we get money only at the end of the year when we get our sheep. So that is why people share posts .. There is no problem with those dying (NB ... sentence not making sense)

1521   When people share posts, one buys food when the other buys...

1540   There is medicine for the stock. We struggle to buy it. The lambs suffer from many types of sickness, they need a persistent man to look after them.

Tsietse comes along

1620   Mashaile says it's windy and cold today

1637   nice shot of sekaunkola and sleeping dog

mutterings, shots of herders on stone wall.

Appendix 3

Group discussion

TAPE 6

001   Herders - Jareteng

004   Remaketse (R): Do you have any comments on what you have seen in the film?

046   *Hache*! We don't have any comments.

050   (Herder on left): We don't have any comments? Yes. Is it because you understood what was being said? Yes. What did they say to start with. Maybe you will make us agree with what we do not know. No. I do not make you agree with what you do not understand ... (Herder left) What did you understand from it? I understood what they said.

112   Chere: What did they say, we want to hear from you.

114   I was still there. You do not have to answer for those people who might be making mistakes.

120   Did you not understand what they were talking about?

131   Chere: I agree with what people said that the animals must graze on the grazing land (*makhulo*), in a good way, truly.

144   (Herder on left): Yes, but did you hear they can graze but we should be aware that of the quality of the grazing and whether the number of posts should be increased. So what can you say about the point?

158   Chere: The number of posts will increase.

208   (Herder left): It will increase? Yes. Being aware of quality of grazing ... Yes. That will satisfy the animals.

209   Chere: The animals, because the Basotho nation is growing, so they will increase and the number of posts will increase.

217   (Herder right): Where will they graze?

219   Chere: They will graze, in this matter the Basotho must limit their animals.

225   everyone speaking

229   They should be limited to how many?

230   To 200.

235   Yours only. Yes

237   (Herder on right): Will it be right for all of us to have 200?

243   Chere: No, that will not happen.

244   (Herder on right): That will not happen?

249   Chere: You will not have 200 all of you.

253   (Herder right): Yes, even if it's like that, that we all do not have 200, will the grazing still be good?

300   Chere: Yes (Herder right): Yes, it will still be there.

305   Chere: If everyone has 200 there will still be good grazing

310   (Remaketse question) Chere: ...how will the government prove that people own 200 or 300? Will the range officials come to check?

343   (Herder left): Ntate, if I understand what you are saying, when the first government officials come, they will find that we have 200 so they will not need to come a second time because they know we are keeping to the limit. But the second lot of officials will need to come to prove for themselves. But we will still not exceed 200.

415   (Herder right): What will they do with the offspring because they will exceed the number. What will they do with it?

421   (Herder p/hat): The animals, if they are limited to that number ... (interjections) ... with the offspring. Say you have 100 ewes so they will make 300. Do you take the other share and sell it. 200 still remains.

447   Chere: Yes, you bank the money.

450   Chere: And use it for your own purposes.

450   (Herder right): Yes, you say that, but I am not willing to sell my animals.

455   (Herder hat): But you must understand if it's the law you must follow it. That's all.

504   (Herder right): Yes, I understand that will be the ... because if it was not the law it could not happen...

514   Chere: Because we see the land is diminishing (*qepha*) but the people are increasing 200 is enough for the land ... 200 is enough if everyone has 200 ... even if the people are many, when he reaches 200 he must see what he must do. The land will be sufficient.

540   (Herder right) So we who want 300 will become dissatisfied?

542   Chere: Hache. But you will be dissatisfied by mistake because you still see how the land is.

549   (Herder left): It's a fight for the land (to improve)

551   Chere says yes, it's a fight for the land, for how they must graze

558   (Herder right): Yes, I understand how much land is available for the herds. But if I want 300 will we be dissatisfied?

609   (peak hat): Excuse me, you understand if you are given this limit, we are not looking at one's life, we are looking at everyone's life generally, (herder right) Yes ... (peak hat) for everyone...

628   I want to have 300 knowing my own life, because I know how many people I support. I will find 200 is too little for my life...

636   Chere: I can say to you, I want to add on what you said as a mosotho. If you have 200, having bought a ram, having improved your sheep, they are enough for you to feed, even having cultivated fodder for them, you will know the way to feed them according to how you know the country is.

709   that is limit for yourself to feed them, so tell me if you have a 1000 and this man has a 1000, and that one has a 1000, where will a 1000 graze?

722   (Herder right) I don't say a 1000. I say look, if we have more than another, sometimes say I support two families, so I must have 300 to support them. So what must I do ... (interjection) will 200 not be enough? ... Yes, 200 is not enough. Maybe it will be enough to satisfy me with my two families. I need to have 300 to support those two families.

745   (voice) If you have nothing, no animals or anything, can't you survive?

753   Can't I survive? But you can see I cannot survive but now we are talking on this point ... (interjection) Cannot you survive? (interjection) Yes, we must agree on this point. Yes, but with difficulty. You survive with difficulty. But you will still survive, not so. Yes, but no one likes to live like that, with difficulty.

813   Chere: Ntate Lifomo, I will ask you again. Can you see when you get more and more stock wealth, can you see that you will end up having things that will fall into the rivers? Not knowing what their use is. (Lifomo interjects) We must agree here.

832   Chere: Do you see what is being fought for is the land, it is diminishing ... it is diminishing (amidst interjections). If you walk over there, to that ridge, you will see that the land is diminishing because there are many posts.

849   Lifomo: Now you own stock because you want to live. Yes, thank you.

855   Lifomo: and you say you will live from them. ...Yes, they will, I thank you.

904   R: What do you say about this argument? (to old man)

915   (red hat) .. whether accept 200 or we can exceed 300 or stop at 400.

921   Ntsitsoane: Me, I was looking at my work. Ntate, the argument that I see I think everybody is looking at his own family. No one can say he is not looking at his

family. According to the government policy (*leano la muso*), the land is not the same as in the past. There is a shortage of land. (955) The breeding of stock is not the same as in the past, it is heavy now than in the past. In the past the land was (*iketla*) in good condition/well.

1007   Many people migrated from their places to Mokhotlong because of the good grazing. But today, our land is being overloaded (*imeloa*) by stock. Look now, in some parts it is being eroded. That is why it must be reserved for summer, it must be reserved for winter. (1026) This is for the animals to get good grazing in those places at the time. (1035) Repeats again ... and (1041) Not to overload yourself for people to say you are rich. (1047) It has been limited for the animals to prosper.

1051   It has been limited for the animals to prosper. (1056) And it has been said that we must have government rams and bulls for them to prosper.

1120   R: Can you remind me of these people who have offices at Malefiloane. Range management officials. Have these officials come to you? Here at the cattleposts? Yes. Yes, they come. R: When you go to them what do they say? ... They say we must protect the land (pointed to E side). Cattleposts like this people shouldn't graze there and we don't have to burn the grass because we are decreasing the grazing.

1229   R: So what do they want to do to protect such things? No. they didn't explain to us. R: What do you say you can do to improve the grazing? We have to stop burning grass and stop grazing on eroded land. R: What more? (Clarification from herder, red hat. Repeats answer again) R: Didn't they say they wanted to divide the land into fenced pieces? They talked of that but they never said how they were going to do that.

1329   R: Did you like what they said? Of fencing the land? Hache, no I don't like it. R: Do others like it? No. Of fencing the land? We are not happy with it.

1400   (Asks R how are they going to fence, and how is the fencing going to improve the grazing land) R: No, I don't know. I'm asking you people who attend the meetings. Who goes for the meetings of fencing. Yes. Do you understand, interchange...

1440   (Speaks to R) Although you say you don't know if they fence are our animals going to be inside the fences. R: Yes. How much land is going to be fenced? R: (shakes head) I have to ask you because you attend the meeting. I'm not happy with the fencing.

1529   R: Are you happy with having anything to say. In Sani they made a reserved pasture for three years and must do the same thing here if want to improve the land. The pasture will improve if it is reserved. No animals will graze here. (Old one asks) Do you mean Sani has been fenced? No, it's not fenced. Nothing has been done on Sani but it has been reserved. Not for animals to graze but to accumulate much grass. So for our land to accumulate much grass it needs to be reserved like Sani. (1629) Where must they graze. Animals. They will choose a place for them to graze. You have got cattlepost. Old man asks where can't you find animals. (Red hat asks old man) While your animals are here are there animals on your winter posts. (Old man says) Do you understand those posts are for winter. (Old man, Champagne, says) Should the animals spend two years grazing on the winter posts. (Man with horse says) Lesotho is large so can take the land from this ridge to Langelboletsi valley and reserve it. (1706) From Mokhotlong to Sani we graze our animals there.

1709　So when there's lots of grass here we come from that side to this side. R: Can you give the old man a chance to speak? Champaigne: I find it better when they don't increase the number of posts if it is the correct number of posts for the land, so this sheep is enough for this pasture ... much it's enough not to increase the number of ... cap. Excuse me, the reason is that I'm born here in Mokhotlong. I'm my father's son. He brings me up so I'm old enough. Now I've grown, I've got my own stock, so where do I have to go. Other guy says where I will be given the site (as if is the leather hat) Leather hat ... so as not to increase the number of posts I've got my stock. (Old man says) Where are you going to be given a site. (Leather hat says) So that the number of posts will not increase... confusion, interruption...

1905　(Leather hat) If I am given a site I increase the number of posts now what must they do with me, with my stock, because I have no post but have animals. (Old man says) You will stay at your father's post. We are separated, we are separated from my father. R: Why should you ask the old man? What do you say yourself? (Young guy) No. I am supposed to ask him if I'm going to understand because the old man says the number of posts is enough here. That is why he asks him, because he is old enough, has his own stock and wants to stay on his own so that will he do with him ... repeating questions etc. ...

TAPE 7

Old man knitting. Do you know how much it was limited for the person who owns small stock (sheep, goats)? Leather hat says yes. (Old man) How much? (Leather) 100. (Old man says) But at first they said fifty. (Small guy says) It was even broadcast. (Old man says) It was enough for you to be able to feed them. You buy a ram just like now ... when people talk of fences, whether it satisfies them. Yes, people are satisfied. When this idea first came it was said that it it will be where our animals will be protected when we put rams and bulls when we want to improve our stock the rams will be given their own camp and the bull will be on their camp where people will be told how much to pay to breed with the bull/ram (nehala). When they first fenced at Malfilwani they were not based on improving the grazing they were for improving the stock with rams and bulls. Don't you know where in Malfilwani where the fences are? Yes, we know. (Old man) So there will be herders and doctors for that stock. (Red hat asks) Are all stock going to be bred there? Old man says yes. Repeats.

214   R: What about here at the cattlepost? Didn't they say they wanted to fence as well? (Old man) It will be fenced and that will be starting improvement of pastures. They said this side will be reserved graze that side, when grass diminished we come this side. 255

315   R: How did you feel about this? (Old man) ... I don't understand/like it because that will be the law and we will have to obey it because it is the law. (Small guy says) Does it satisfy you? (Old man) No. (Young guy) How many would satisfy you? (Old man) I should have as many as I can, maybe 300. (433) even 4000, I will sell them when they get many.

452   (Man with horse) Chere says where will your 4000 graze? (Old man) I would like to have 4000 but according to the law I will have to obey. (Blue hat) Now you have come to my point. I have power to feed my 300. (Old man) We must speak one at a time. I have spoken enough. I will give other people a chance.

526   (Young guy) Have we agreed to limit our stock? (Old man) No. It is only because we Basotho live under law ... repeats. (Young guy) We agree. (Champaigne) 200 is enough. (Young guy) We agree. (Chere) Yes. 200 is enough. all agree. (Young guy) What do you say Mekete (Leather hat). Should we stop at 200 or exceed. (Mekete)I can see the land is no longer strong, there is a big difference since 1981 when I first came here. It was strong in the past but now it has diminished, which proves the land is diminishing. There are many animals so the land has to diminish and the posts are many so that is why I think the stock must be limited and we must stop at 200. (Blue hat) I now understand. (Mekete) When I first came here there were few posts (points) there are two cattleposts on this side, two up there and one on this side.

Champaign tells Tim where post were and new ones (948) ...

1050   R: When you say stock should be limited to 200 do you think other people should hire others? Yes. R: Should they still pay them 12 sheep Yes. (Young guy) Some of us are being paid six sheep, some eight, and some twelve, isn't it so. Some people being paid money, some people with a cow or horse or a donkey. I get satisfied. (1148) Some can take five sheep and the rest in money to make that twelve so what do others say. Yes, we agree.

1205   Chere: To hire one another is to help each other. If we hire one another and you have 200 and you put a ram and you get the offspring you will pay your herder with the offspring and that is to help each other ... repeats.

1249   R: Did you hear you will have to pay tax for your animals? Clarify your question. R repeats question. (Mekete) They said it was set that horse, donkey, mule, cow would be five Rand. Sheep and goat would be fifty cents. R: Why do you have to pay tax? (Mekete) Because there must be limitations ... repeats ...because sometimes it will be heavy to pay the tax for my stock because there are many. And now I will have to sell some of them, again it has been said that the tax will improve the grazing lands.

1440   Do you encourage it or don't you like it? (Mekete) No, I don't like it. Why? Young guy repeats. (Mekete) I don't understand it because I don't find its importance. Young guy says he doesn't understand why should they pay tax for the grass, the grass for the animals because it's there for them to graze.

1543   (Mekete)What is painful about this tax is we have to pay tax for the animals which is in the form of money, so we shear them to get money (wool). It doesn't bring in much money. So with what do we have to pay tax and survive with. (Young guy) We need to survive like those people who make us pay tax so the money is being eaten by them. (Mekete) With what shall we pay tax and with what shall we survive, that is death.

1629   R: How does this dissatisfy you because you said the money will be used for improving the stock and pastures? So I don't understand, are animals not going to be improved or what?

1645   It dissatisfies me. The reason is where am I going to get the money to pay tax because I have no money.

1653   (another voice) You understand. He is happy with it but there is no money.

1655   R: So what can you say? Do they have to raise the wool prices? Various voices: Yes, so that we can pay tax.

1708   R: How can the wool prices be raised, because there is no market. You understand that Lesotho itself takes the wool and sells it to somewhere else? Yes. So it is being bought at the market price there. Yes. (1727) The weight of the size of my hand is bough for a Rand. So how much do you want it to be bought for? R10? So that you get much money?

1739   (Herder left) Ntate, I can say to you, you know the things called cheques by which we get the money, so when you look at where the wool is being bought you will find that the wool is being bought for much money.

1755   I am not arguing with you about it being bought for a Rand, but you find though it was bought for much money when it (the money) reaches you, it is not as much as when it was being bought.

1805   R: Where do you think the money is being taken out/cut (*khaoloa*)?

1808   It's the government.

1811   R: And the government has not explained to you why it has taken the money?

1816   Chere: Here at Malefiloane there was .... discussing the issue of money. They said, the people who made the pitso (the officials), what is the concern of the audience/people about the money being eaten when they (the government) had taken their fathers' (money). Is that when they have something to say about their money being eaten. So that's it? (*nyoee nyoee*) They (the officials) said this there at Malefiloane. Is that the place when you can say so that's it we have eaten and finished your grandfathers' (money).

[Translation: The officials at the Pitso asked people about this matter of money but in fact the government had already eaten our fathers' money. So is this the occasion to discuss the question of the money when in fact it has already gone]

1848   they said "You can take these sheep and shear them for yourselves" (i.e. the people can go and find their own market). So with what are we going to pay tax because they say they have eaten the money. Those people are killing us.

1908   You know, last year ... (1910) I was at Mokhapoung, we, the association (WGA) decided to make a strike because it is useless there is no money. R: How did you decide to strike?

1927   Because it was a long time since we had sheared our sheep and no money had come in and our households were dying. The money did not arrive. (1935) (interjection: we don't have to send our wool there). Ah, because the officials work as if we are hired (to them) and yet the animals are ours.

1947   interjection (Blue hat) The strike will be that we do not send our wool there

1952   interjection: and to strike about our money which is being eaten

1955   No, wait, there was a reason behind that. The mistake was not with the market (point) the wool goes via here, and it reaches the market, it is bought. So when it leaves the market the money goes via Maseru. It stays there a long time (2019) interjections: that is where it is being eaten.

2022   So the problems were that it was not clear why the money did not arrive.

TAPE 8

Old man knitting...

0034   R: How old are you? 19. Do you want to go on herding or do you wan to change? Yes, I want to herd. R: Same question to other boy. Yes. R: Don't you want to do another work? No. I tried to attend school but my father didn't have the money so I said I will continue herding.

0104   R: Is there anyone among you who has been to the Theba office seeking a job? There at Mokhotlong? Yes. No, I've never been. Yes, I have been seeking jobs there. R: So what happened? Couldn't make any progress so continued herding. When was this? Last year.

0122   R: Do you have any explanation as to why there is no work? Yes, it was explained to me that there is no work and there are many people on the mines. They said they didn't need any more people so I found there is no work on the mines, that is why I had to herd.

0151   It has been broadcast on radio that there is no work on the mines. Chere: Let's finish up this thing of tax because I don't understand it as a Basotho. Now the prices of goods are high in the shops when we have 200 even this old blanket I'm putting on is hard to find. For 200 you can only get three bags of maizemeal. So with what are we now going to pay tax and with what are we going to live.

0247   R: So what must be done with this tax? It must be done away with so you don't have to pay tax. ...repeats about five times. So what can be done is that everybody owns a sock of the same limitation. Young guy asks these questions you asking us, are our complaints going to be solved as we say we don't like this tax.

0341   R: (replies) The film is being done for people who don't know about you to see what your problems are so they can help you. (Other guy says) things like tax must be stopped so we can live well.

400   (Mekete) If the prices at shops were low it would be possible to pay tax so ask yourself with us being loaded with high prices and tax is that not death. R: You must look at life as something that is steady/stable, life changes. (Tim) Didn't you say that officials from Malefiloane haven't visited here. (437) waffle ... (Other guy says) haven't they come?

500   Tim asks little guy what do you want to say. No we once saw them passing by, riding on their horses but they never said anything to us. There is nothing they said as to what they are doing but I don't know if they ever talked to the old people like Ntate Ntsitsoane.

545   (Old guy says) They just passed by going this way. They went by and passed by that is why all of us don't know anything about them. It is rumoured that they were coming to check to see if posts are many/crowded but I didn't take this from their mouths.

638   (Young guy) But the way they came as I saw doesn't agree with what you were saying that they were coming to check the posts, because when you are this side you cannot see them.....

Appendix 4

Motebong (At The Cattle Post)

First Draft

00.00   no picture, music from shebeen, concertina.
   10   Steve in edit suite (March '91- VHS)
   20   Driving, reflective shot in side mirror (Feb '91-VHS)
   30   Tanki saddling horse (Feb '91-VHS)
   39   Loading pack donkeys   "   "
   53   Mountain scenery from village near Mokhotlong (Feb-VHS)
   55   Tim on horse, cross river with donkeys (Feb- VHS)
1.26   Team riding along ridge, mountain views (Feb-VHS)
   48   Setting up camera/interview at Loi's post (March, Hi8)

1.58   Mashaile leaning on kraal wall (LB5)
       (4.09 cut away to M. driving sheep into kraal-Hi8)

My name is Mashaile Kapa from Moseli Ntsiking. I grew up herding horses and after that I went to school up to standard 6. I had to leave school because my father was no more working.And I said to my father, no, I am going to work. I got hired by his uncle herding cattle at home. If I remember well it was probably 11 years I stayed with my uncle then I went away from my uncle to initiation school. When I came back I went to Thabang at Khaole's place. I worked a year there. He paid me with a cow and I went away and got hired by Thabo Tsita at Thabang. I stayed until now this is the fifth year being at Thabo's place. I have now 37 livestock. I think in the future I want to marry, having my own building (in village). I'm still young, 23 years old.

4.12   Mashaile by kraal wall (LB5)

I desire that in the future my stock will not exceed 70. When they reach 70, I exchange the ewes for hammels. I sell the hammels to get money. This thing for accumulating wealth in animals but not getting food from them but God has made the lamb for one to live with. But this is to argue with God.

I wish he helps me to have worked by the time I marry because here I am in a wilderness, having no female company (having left girl's saliva). Her it is cold. Its desolate where Christ was born.

5.07   Sebokoane Kao - close up, sitting on sofa (July '90- VHS)

My father didn't send me to school. I have been herding. I send my children to school.

- Why?

For them to know how to read and write. I don't know, animals are diminishing. Education lasts longer than animals because it does not rot. When a person dies the education dies with him.

5.48   Livestock are a black man's life. A black man's life is animals because a black man does not know how to keep money. Money is you white people's because you know it. So that is why I say my son must know about animals and money but know most about animals.

6.30   What is Moqeneheloa's job now?

- He works at the bank of Lesotho.

6.46   Sebokaone's herder - in hut (March '91 - LB5)

I was herding my father's stock before I came to Sebokoane. He hired me from my home and I came to him under employment agreements. I was hired in 1989.

7.36   -did you attend school?

-Yes, up to standard 2.

- Why did you leave school?

- I like to herd sheep because I saw people who herded before me were gaining and I thought it was a waste of time to be schooling because I would not get animals to get married with (bohali).

8.04   Mashaile, group interview, close up March '91 - LB1)

We do not know really what the younger boys' opinions are on not attending school but they don't want to say whether it was their father's who made them come up here. (Repeats himself).

8.37   -(Mashaile) Why did you come here?

-(young boy with cap) I was herding, I did not like school, there was nobody to herd and I was not interested in school.

-(other young boy) I have been attending school meanwhile we had no-one to herd the cattle at the post.

-(Mashaile) So your parents took you out of school?

-Yes.

-Did you feel angry about it?

-No I did not feel angry.

9.01   Thaole,(blue hat) in group interview (March '91 - LB1)

This type of herding is no good for these young boys because they are people who should be learning some work and attending schools learning about knitting and saddlery. Because of a lack of herders it is why they are up here herding. Ideally, many people should be herding who are old enough and have children so then its a mistake for the young boys to herd. They should get an education from the start. They should come here herding when they are old enough when they are closer to my age.

10.01   Lebosa, (floppy hat), group interview

We left our families because we wanted t have stock to support my family. When I ask people with stock to help they say when we have been working you have been watching, so work for yourself and get stock to support your family. That is why we are up here herding.

-(Thaole), that is true, they are bringing you to the way, they need your help then they can share their stock with you.

10.43 Lebosa

It has been a long time and I have forgotten. I started when I was young. I herded, I even got married while being a herder at the posts. I went to Johannesburg. In Johannesburg I worked until 1977 and I came back to herd until now.

11.10 Mashaile, group interview

There is no work because we are too many. That is why you will find many of us herding.

11.26 cut away, sheep in valley pan to view up valley

12.04 Loi, close up, group interview March '91 - LB3)

Ntate, I wake up in the morning. I go to the spring. I draw water come back and cook papa. Then I drive my sheep back into the kraal. I milk. After that I eat. Then I go and gather bushes sometimes until the sun sets. I stop when I have brought my sheep into the kraal.

12.25 Noah Nkuni, Loi's employer,full body shot, incl R. (March 91 - LB9)
-R Is it easy or hard to find herders?
-It is hard, it is hard.
-Can you find experienced herders or new ones?
-These two herders satisfy me like Loi.

12.40 pan of two herders, village, back to Noah (LB9)

I have been his guardian from when he was very young. He was given to me to bring up. I started by just giving him sheep taking him as my child.

13.09 Loi, group interview, medium shot (LB3)

It can be said that I am young and fit to earn six sheep. But he can send me wherever he wants, even if it is cold while his children stay at home but after that he pays me six sheep. That is what dissatisfies me.
-R. Are you dissatisfied inside or have you spoken to your employer?
-it dissatisfies but because of problems, I fear to tell him. I think he will fire me.
-Why don't you tell your parents that you are dissatisfied with your pay.
-Hache, I am still thinking of telling them.

13.43 -How much do you think a person of your age should be paid each year?
-12 sheep because we are equal.

13.52 Noah Nkuni, full shot to medium, in village (LB9)

He is trustworthy, he grew up here.
-R. Do you pay him in sheep or money?
-I pay him in sheep.
-R. How many.
-I started by paying 4 up to 5 or 6 sheep, now I am going to pay him 12.
-R. Is it good to pay someone of his age 12 sheep.
-According to Basotho custom I find it good. Everyone of that age is being paid 12 sheep.

14.35 cut away: Loi with brushwood by hut, goes in (Hi8?)
   57 goats moving by kraal,
   08 sheep near cliffs, boy milking, sekhaunkola music
   18 Sekhaunkola player, music
   26 fat man spinning wool
   37 three herders by Mashaile's hut, pan to two young boys sitting on stones (one with bright blanket)
   59 checking sheep in Mashaile's kraal, (boy with bright blanket is central)
16.08 Loi and Mashaile bringing sheep past hut

16.14 Mashaile cooking in hut at night (march '91 - Hi8,3)
   34 M. picking up pot
   47 T. Does Loi hunt for eland?
      -Yes, in Natal, with dogs

17.01 Old man, boy and T. side view in hut, smoky
      - are you paid
      - no,yes, its our job, we teach and we study

17.17 Young boy next to old man
      T. voice, film is like bioscope
      -(boy) I once saw TV in Maseru

17.35 shot of book with Trojan horse,pan to old man(Hi8,3)

      -M.(voice), look at him, he just putting his hands on his waist. They are driving it and his hands are just on his waist.
      -(old man), what is this?
      -its a war.
      -(boy), is the horse standing on planks?
      -No, its made of planks

17.58 Old man and M. stirring pot
      (old man), why don't you make a tripod?
      -I don't know, truly, but you see up here at the posts we cannot find wire easily.
      -There is a lot of wire down at the dip.

18.20 M. turning papa in pot with stick

18.48 M. on what he eats
      -Each day I eat papa and milk

-Sheep or cows milk?
-Cows milk, in winter I eat only papa
In winter I eat only papa, ntate Alotsi
-T. and fish?
-papa only..yes there are fish here, and eland meat
-Eland meat? where do you get it?
-by the cliffs
-where?
-by the cliffs

19.36 old man sitting, M.'s voice then pan to M and back to old man (Hi8, 3)

-which posts were here when you were young?
-what?
-cattleposts, how many were there in Langalabalele and Jareteng valleys?
-This was Ramorebeli's the top one was Tlaka's
- are you talking of Mokhotso's post?
- No Sello went there from here
Noah Nkuni's post was Monokoase's
- what about higher up the valley? were there any posts there?
-They were there
-where was Sebokaone's post?
-I do not know Sebokoane's post -do you know where Hlaaaha's post is?
-Yes
-There is another in front of it, that was Ramotau's post
-I can see that's where Sebokoane's post is and there is another below it
-Sebokaone's is above. Yes just above the river.

21.26 T. Long ago did people have two posts, one to use in winter?
- No, people only had one post, just like you Mashaile, you do not move from here.
Even us, we used to stay in winter at the cattlepost
-M. in winter and summer.
-(old man) People mae two posts because of the restrictions placed on grazing area, and a small boy like this, he cannot stay far alone, and gather bushes for fires, the snow will force him inside.
That over there was Macheli's post, there are two new posts near there.
- there where Nkoane and Ntala have their posts
- Ntala and Nkoane, Oh.. that was Macheli's post.
- and Thaole's post
-Its very old, it was his father's post

22.45 Thaole, standing alone half body shot (March '91,LB4)
(cutaways 24.23; 25.45 to valley scenery)
(close up on Thaole,26.42)
In this valley of Jareteng and Langalabalele there were only four (other) posts. (points) Moruti Mosese's post up this valley of Jareteng. (points) Lebopo's post down this valley. (points) Mashaile's place was Tseko's post and (points) Polisa's post up there. The fifth

one was my father's and I now own his post. The posts were only that much in this valley. There was lots of grass (points) the grass was better and Seboku covered this hill. (Points) on this side Letsiri covered the hill. There was few firewood bushes. Lelingoana grew close to the river here and Sehalala also close to the river. There was much moqoboqobo, it grew like trees along the river as you can see it now, its this one I'm holding. Now the land has changed because it has not got the same grass as we had in the past. It is few and there is no Letsiri. Firewood bushes have covered the whole land over there. There is much wealth and people are many. It is necessary that we join the improvement groups right away to get advice from the chiefs and Agric people to bring us peace.

(cut away)

In the past people kept their grazing well because not many people were herding up here and the wealth was with few people, and the villages were not as huge as now.

27.04   Francis Ntlela, by vehicle, Malefiloane, July '91,LB3)

Since 1971 the rangelands have been deteriorating...

27.43   change of shot to close up
I can put it this way....

29.10   group shot, group interview at Loi's post (March '91, LB1)
M. calls to Lebosa, - come over here, Mr Lebosa.

29.14   Lebosa, close up

Even if the government tries to improve the grazing lands, as I look at it the land will never be improved because the number of livestock is much higher than in the past. Look there, there, there. But now, if you go around here there is a post, there, a post. So by the time they try to reserve (ho Beha) the grazing the animals should be on one side to allow improvement on the other. They depart one side having burnt the grass. when the go to the other side they burn again. There is no other way the grazing will be improved because of the large number of livestock.

30.00   Herders in jareteng watching demo film by tent, back view
12 shot from front, herders watching (music from concertina)

30.17   Jareteng group interview, Ntsikoane (old man knitting, shot broadens out to whole group.

voice   (Hdr on right) we don't have any comment.
        -(Hdr left) we don't have any comment?
        -Yes.
        -Is it because you understood what was being said.
        -Yes.
        -What did they start with. Maybe you will make us agree with what we do not know
        -No. I do not make you agree with what you do not understand
        -what did you understand from it?

-I understood what they said

-(Chere) What did they say? we want to hear from you.

-I was there. You do not have to answer for those people who might be making mistakes

- (Hdr left?) did you not understand what they were talking about?

- (Chere) I agree with what people said that the animals must graze on grazing land in a good way, truly.

-(Hdr left) Yes but did you hear that they can graze but we should be aware of the quality of grazing and whether the number of posts should be increased. So what can you say on that point.

-(Chere) the number of post will increase

-(Hdr left) It will increase?

-Yes

-even being aware of quality of grazing

-Yes.. it will satisfy the animals

-(Chere) the animals, because Basotho nation is growing so they will increase and the number of posts will increase

-(hdr right) Where will they graze?

-(Chere) they will graze, in this matter basotho must limit their animals

-interjections-

-(hdr right?) they should be limited to how many?

- to 200

-Your only?

-Yes

-(hdr right) will it be alright for all of us to have 200?

-(Chere) No, that will not happen

-(hdr left) that will not happen

-(Chere) you will not have 200 all of you.

-(hdr right) Yes, even if it is like that, that we all do not have 200, will the grazing still be good?

-(Chere) Yes

-(hdr right) Yes?

-(Chere) it will still be there. If every one has 200 there will still be good grazing.

32.44   change of shot to herder on left with cigarette, black cap herder speaks.

-(black cap) the animals, if they are limited to that number.. (interjections)... with the offspring, say you have 100 ewes so they will make 300, so you take the other share and sell it. 200 still remains.

-(Chere) Yes, and you bank the money. and use it for your own purposes

-(Hdr right) Yes, you say that but I am not willing to sell my animals

-(black cap) but you must understand if it is law you must follow it. That's all.

-(hdr right) Yes, I understand that will be the law because if it was not law it could not happen

34.57   change shot, Chere talking with hand in front of mouth

-(Chere) because we see the land is diminishing (qepha -there is a shortage of land) but people are increasing, 200 is enough for the land. 200 is enough even if the people are many when he reaches 200 he must see what he must do. The land will still be sufficient.

-(hdr right) so we who want 300 will become dissatisfied

-(Chere) Hache, but you will be dissatisfied by mistake because you still see how the land is

-(hdr left) it is a fight for the land (to improve)

-(Chere, Yes its a fight for the land, for how they must graze.

-(hdr right) Yes, I understand how much land is available for the herds. But if I want 300 will we be dissatisfied.

-(black cap) excuse me, you understand if you are given this limit, we are not looking at one's life, we are looking at everyone's life generally....

-(hdr right) Yes

-(black cap) ...for everyone.

(cut)-(Chere) Mr Lifomo, I will ask you again. Can you see that when you get more and more stock wealth can you see that you will end up having things that fall in the rivers, not knowing what their use is?.. (interjection by Lifomo (hdr right)... We must agree here. Do you see what is being fought for is the land. It is diminishing. It is diminishing .. (interjections)... If you walk over there to that ridge you will see that the land is diminishing because there are many posts.

35.33 change shot to Ntsikoane (herder knitting)

-(hdr left) Mr Ntsikoane?

-(Ntsikoane) Me? I was looking at my work. Ntate, the argument that I see i think everyone is looking at his own family. No one can say he is not looking at his family. According to the government policy, the land is not the same as in the past, there is a shortage of land. The breeding of stock is not the same as in the past, it is heavier now than in the past. In the past the land was in good condition/well.

Many people migrated from their places to Mokhotlong because of good grazing. But today our land is being overloaded (imeloa) by stock. Look now, in some parts it is being eroded. That is why it must be reserved for summer, it must be reserved for winter. This is the time for the animals to get good grazing in those places at the time.

36.53 wide shot of group

-(Chere) page 24 of recoded script.

39.01 group scene, Remaketse's voice then he comes into picture

-(Hdr left) Ntate I can say to you, you know those things called cheques by which we get the money, so when you look at where the wool is being bought you will find that the wool is being bought for much money

-R. I am not arguing with you about it being bought for a rand but you find it was bought for much money when it reaches you it is not as much as when it was being bought. Where do you think the money is being taken out (khoala). Its the government.

-Yes

-R. and the government has not explained to you why it has taken the money?

-(Chere) Here at Malefiloane there was a pitso discussing the issue of money. The government officials asked the people about the problem of money, but why? in fact the government had already eaten our father's money. So why discuss money when it has already gone. Then they said, you can take these sheep and shear them for yourselves (i.e. find your own market) So what are we going to pay tax with because they say they have eaten the money. Those people are killing us.

-(black cap) You know last year I was at Mokhapoung. We the association (WGA) decided to strike because it is useless, there is no money.

-R. How did you decide to strike?

-because it was a long time since we had sheared our sheep and no money had come in and our households were dying. The money did not arrive...(interjection) we don't have to send our wool there...Ah, the officials work as if we are hired to them yet the animals are ours.

-(Hdr right[Lifomo]) The strike will be that we do not send our money there .. and to strike about our money being eaten.

-(black cap) No there was a reason behind that. The mistake was not with the market. (points) the wool goes from here and it reaches the market, it is bought. So when it leaves the market the money goes via Maseru, that is where it is being eaten. So the problems were that it was not clear why the money did not arrive.

41.50	pan from horses to shearing shed at Mokhotlong
58	inside shed, pan across shed, shearers at work, stop on blue overall man shearing a goat
42.18	another shearer, close up of bleating goat
26	back to original shearer- close up shearing belly
30	shearer puts sheared goat onto its feet, sends it running towards door
40	man picks up mohair from floor, carries it over to grading table
43.04	close up of hands grading mohair, widens out to women grading, throwing mohair
19	shot of in, mohair dropping onto pile
21	outside shed, R and mike in view plus interviewee

R. Why are wool prices low?

- For a long time we had good wool and mohair prices but since last year we received unusual cheques, the wool prices were very low. We asked many questions to the government about the low wool prices and the prices being low we did not receive our second payment for mohair, it being said that our mohair is at the border not yet bought. Its been said that the reason is the Gulf War. The second reason is the countries which bought much of the mohair like China are no longer using mohair. Even this year we are shearing but we do not know what the prices are and whether our wool will be bought. Maybe the government will try and help them to find a market for the wool but we don't know whether this will happen.

45.28   Mashaile herding sheep, throws stone, drive sheep towards kraal.

46.06   Mashaile by kraal

-Hache, I want to go on herding. I herd and after that after three years I will stop. I don't want to stay not doing anything. I will still come to the posts.

(cut) Look at these mountains and plateaux, they are silent. Now I don't know about these people who go down to the villages at the beginning of May. It is only me who stays along with Sebokoane's herder who is up at the head of the valley, and Mokhotos's herder un by these cliffs. But all around here it is just me.

(cut) The harshness for a person staying here is such that sometimes when you get home people think that you are anti-social (khopo). But its not that because by the time people have gone down to the villages one has spent about a month not speaking to anybody. Now when you arrive there, people speak to you too much and you get tired. And you think all the people are staring at you but its not that but its because you have been away for a long time.

(cut) The month of June, there is frost. May and June are the coldest months. Truly there is a lot of frost.

48.15   R and herder at different post (Feb field trip) (SVHS)

-R. is it cold here in winter?

- Hey , the cold here, in winter, ay, ay, ay... when you get home (from the posts) and you are not even interested in women, then you know it is not alright. At home it, (the penis) doesn't rise. Aikona. Well I must go now, Hey, its just warm this month.

48.42   Mashaile by kraal (March '91,LB5)

This wilderness wants a person who renounces himself (itela) someone who enjoys the sweetness of life will not stay here.

Appendix 5

Motebong (At The Cattle Post)

Structure Of First Draft

Introduction

showing that is a team travelling to make a film
2 min music
1.38 min imagery

Body

Format	Message
1) close up body shot	introduce herders
single person	Mashaile, main character
subject speaks	a herder's history, education to work
no questions	a herder's plans for future
one cut away	a herder's loneliness, desires
exterior	description: cp areas as desolate/wilderness

Time: 3.09 min; cut away approx 20 seconds   1.58 -5.07

2) close up body	- introduce stock owners
& head shots	- Sebokoane Kao
single person	- stock owner's history-education
subject speaks	- plans for own sons
one question asked	- stereotype views; (but well said):
no cut away	- a) importance of education to Basotho
interior	- b) importance of livestock as wealth vis a vis money
	- humour; wealth being both livestock and money

Time 1.41 min 5.07 - 6.46

3) body shot
   single person
   subject speaks
   some questions
   exterior

- Sebokoane's herder
- education and work history
- young herders prefer herding to school

Time: 1.18 min   6.46-8.04

4) group shot
   one subject asking
   questions of others
   pan across from hdr
   to young hdrs
   exterior

- focus on main character, Mashaile
- older herder understanding vis young
  herder
- young herders prefer herding to school
- indication that poverty makes parents
  use children as herders

Time: 57 secs 8.04 -9.01

5) cut/group shot but
   focus on one
   discussion by subjects
   of issue (education)
   subject speaks
   no questions
   exterior

- old men as herders
- Thaole (blue hat)
- older hdrs question use of boys as
  herders
- importance of education but
  different view to Sebokoane

Time: 1.00 min, 9.01 - 10.01

6) cut/group shot but
   focus on two
   face shot
   subject speaks
   another responds
   no questions
   exterior

- film using group interview method
- old men are herders, Lebosa & Thaole
- herders are poor
- men must work
- need for man to show worth before
  people will help
- a herder as a humorous character

Time: 42 sec, 10.01 - 10.43

7) cut/face shot   - continuation of previous talk
    cut to first   - (Lebosa) herders as ex migrants
    subject   - short life history
    subject speaks
    no questions
    exterior

Time: 27 secs, 10.43 - 11.10

8) cut/to another hdr   - bring back main character (M)
    group shot   - continuation of talk on lack of work
    subject speaks   - lack of work forces men to be hdrs
    interjections   - disagreement between hdrs
    no questions
    exterior

Time: 16 secs, 11.10 - 11.26

9) wide shot   - herders look after sheep
    livestock and land   - shows type of landscape for herding
    natural sounds
    exterior

Time: 40 secs, 11.26 -12.04

10) face shot   - introduce another herder (Loi)
    subject speaks   - introduce new topic: daily routine
    no questions   - hdrs live simple life
                     - sheep stay at post at night

Time: 21 secs, 12.04 - 12.25

11) medium shot   - introduce Loi employer
    interviewer & subject   - problem of finding good herders
    cut to pan of location   - what villages look like
    questions/answers   - employer as guardian
    exterior   - stock owner has several herders

Time: 44 secs, 12.25 - 13.09 one cut away to village (at 12.40)

12) medium shot — relation between hdr and employer
    subject speaks — Loi, anger at conditions of employ
    some questions — hdr fears - power of employer
    exterior — introduce pay of herders

Time: 43 secs, 13.09 - 13.52

13) cut back to earlier — continuation of hdr/employer rel.
    close up to medium shot — elaborate pay of herders
    questions — confirm Loi's argument
    exterior — set out norms of payment

Time:43 secs, 13.52 - 14.35

14) subject in his locale — herder leads rough life
    natural sounds — element of anger in hitting bush
    exterior — against hut
    cuts/goats — herders look after goats
    herder milking sheep — herders lifestyle, how survive
    sekhaunkola music — there is local music
    player — hdrs play music/own instruments
    hdr spinning wool — hdr lifestyle
    hdrs by hut — colourful blankets, what hdrs wear
    pan to young boys — gentle impression - boys as herders
    checking sheep in kraal — work of herders
    known subject in view — herders work, re-establish main character

Time: 1.39 min, 14.35 - 16.14

15) interior of hut — nighttime, life inside a post
    pot on fire, hdr cooking — what herders eat, how cook
    natural discourse — film crew showing what goes on
    cuts — naturally, allowing events to unfold
    some questions — researchers in picture
    hdr questions rschr — reflexive
    boy on TV — reflexive,
    book of Trojan horse — hdrs or rschrs have books?

106

	- hdrs aware of events beyond locale
	- some hdrs can read/limited education of hdrs
	- humour
old man speak to M	- naturalness of film event
on tripod	- living conditions, resource availability

Time: 2.06 min, 16.14 - 18.20

16) interior continuation	- continuation of context
interview	- change to interview situation
subject speaks	- hdr clarify what eat
	- introduce the unusual (eland plus poaching)

Time: 1.16 min, 18.20 - 19.36

17) continuation of context	- subjects interview each other
medium shot/pan	- old herder has knowledge
	- history of posts
cut/researcher asks Q.	- history of post/change in methods
	- reference to subject in film earlier, provides continuity

Time: 3.14 min, 1936 - 22.45

18) body shot	- bring back old herder (Thaole) who
interview	knows history
subject speaks	- history of posts repeated
cutaway to landscape	- change in grazing conditions
	- suggestion of pressure on land
exterior	- need for conservation suggested

Time: 4.19 min, 22.45 - 27.04

19) body shot, interview	- expert speaks (Francis)
subject speaks	- elaborates conservation problem
no questions/cut	- government intervention
	- synopsis of management plans

Time; 2.06 min, 27.04 - 29.10

20) group shot — subjects used to introduce speaker

    return to known film — return of known herder (Lebosa)

    locale

    cut to close up — hdr contest experts view

    subject speaks — herders concerned about land

    no questions — problems

Time: 50 secs, 29.10 - 30.00

21) hdrs watch film — reflexive, film being made

    cut to front view — introduce new group of hdrs

    music same as in intro — reflexive

Time: 17 secs, 30.00 - 30.17

22) individual pan to wide — establish new group

    shot of group

    hdrs talk of film — reflexive, establish issues to be

    hdrs question each other   discussed

    — conservation problems elaborated

    — hdrs arguing, need to limit stock

    — hdrs know the problems

    — old herder view respected

6 cuts 30.17 — stock limitation

      32.44 — argument against limitation/law

      34.57 — stock related to land (overgrazing argument/threat to land)

      35.33 — refer to old herder to summarise, history, ref to summer and winter

      36.53 — page 24 recorded script

      39.01 — argument on wool prices, interviewer is arguing with herders (form of reflexivity), blame on government, herders aware of problems - strike action, problem of wool marketing

Time: 11.33 min, 30.17 - 41.50

23) pan of town to wool — move from mountains to settlement shed

+ 8 secs, cut to	- shearing of goats, hand shearing,
inside shed	men do it
focus on one shearer	- how shearing is done
+20 secs, cut to	- violence to the goat! (harsh
another shearer	imagery)
+8 secs, cut back to	- shearing all over first shearer
+4 secs, cut to finished	- completion of shearing goat, pan of goat run
	out of shed
+10 secs cut, to man	- procedure after shearing introduced
picking up mohair	- slow, care in picking up mohair walk
	introduce next procedure
+24 secs, cut to close	- grading of wool,
up of hands grading	- done by women
widen out to body shot	
of women	- mohair thrown to bins
+15 secs, cut to wool	
landing on pile	- wool collected
interior	

Time: 1.31 min, 41.50 - 43.21
7 cuts (41.58, 42.18, 42.26, 42.30, 42.40, 43.04, 43.19)

24)	interview	- market problems
	single subject focus	
	from view of intrvwr	- interview, official speaks
	interviewer ask one Q.	- herding placed in global context
		- herders affected by Gulf War, international events,
		- stock owning has market risks

Time: 2.09 min, 43.19 - 45.28

25)	Mashaile herding	- back in mountains, herding
	full view, mid distance	- how herder drives sheep
		- re-establish main character

Time: 38 secs, 45.28 - 46.06

26) Mashaile by kraal

subject speaks

exterior

cut

- main character image endorsed, same view as at beginning (completion of circle/film time ending
- plans for future (in context of problems), sombreness
- introduce herders staying up in winter, sense of isolation
- personal fears of village, alienation from village
- introduce coldness of winter

Time: 2.09, 46.06 - 48.15

27) interview
body shots
one question
subject speaks

exterior

- introduce new herder, re-establish interviewer

- coldness of winter, humorous, male oriented society/views

Time: 27 secs, 48.15 - 48.42

28) close up - return to main character,

subject speaks - the loneliness of herding

- completion of film time/circle

End

Appendix 6

Motebong (At The Cattle Post)

Theme And Rhythm Of First Draft Structure

2 min music

1.38 min:	Introduction	travel theme, reflexive- going to make a film, context implied only
3.09 min:	film theme characterisation	life history, harshness of a herder's life (Mashaile)
1.41 min:	context	herders and stock owner, humour, stereotypes (Sebokoane)
1.18 min:	context	relation of herders to stock owners, youth, education (Piti)
57 secs:	elaboration	education of herders, affirm central character (Mashaile)
1.00 min:	elaboration	lack of education as problem, age -old men as herders (Thaole)
42 sec:	continuity/context	general need for herding, poverty (Lebosa)
27 secs:	contextualisation	herding versus wage jobs, migrant labour system (Lebosa), poverty
16 secs:	completion	no work, therefore herd, affirm central character (Mashaile), constraints, poverty
40 secs:	cut away-context	locale of herders, wide spaces - facts
21 secs:	new context	introduce new character (Loi), daily routine
44 secs:	elaboration	relation between stock owner and an individual herder (Noah-Loi), personal relationships
43 secs:	elaboration	herder relation to employer, wage relationship, anger (Loi)
43 secs:	elaboration	wage conditions/norms (Noah), confirmation

1.39 min:	continuity	herders' activities, daily routine, particular characteristics - facts
2.06 min:	continuity/new context	interior living conditions (M)
		reflexive, natural events, humour, wistfulness
1.16 min:	elaboration	interviews, (Mashaile-old man), reflexive, what herders eat - facts
3.14min:	elaboration new context	reflexive interviews (herders interview each other) (M-old man), age, old men have knowledge, history of posts - facts
4.19 min:	contextualisation	history of posts and of vegetation, overgrazing as problem (Thaole)
2.06 min:	elaboration	expert speaks, overgrazing as problem (Francis), herding in context of broader situation
50 secs:	elaboration	questioning of expert view (Lebosa), local concern/doubt
17 secs:	break re-contextualise-	establish new group, reflexive
11.33 min:	elaboration	arguments on overgrazing problem, reflexive (herders argue with each other) (Group), personalities (Chere etc)
1.31 min:	continuity	shearing work procedures - facts
2.09 min:	confirmation	expert interview, herders' problems placed in international context - facts
38 secs:	re-contextualise	herder herding (Mashaile)
2.09 min:	confirmation	herders' plans/aspirations (M), sombreness, alienation, circle of story coming to end
27 secs:	elaboration	coldness of winter, humour, male view of life
15 secs?:	confirmation	central character (Mashaile) harshness of herder's life completion of film time/circle

End

Appendix 7

Second Draft - July 1992

Theme And Rhythm Of Film

1) Need to recognise that we are adopting a subjective approach. Therefore, can make the film as a negative perspective on herding and take licence to emphasise this.

2) Use Mashaile and possibly Mareka as central characters which are offset against others and/or the general group interview discussions.

3) Maintain chronology as much as is possible.

1.30 min	introduction	film researchers identified, introduction of camera to herders, reflexive
3.34 min	herding context harshness	Mashaile herding interspersed with his commentary
2.01 min	herder/employee relationship old men/young boys work/wages	Noah/Loi relationship
1.39	stock owner	Sebokoane on lack of education, stereotype views
1.26 min	herder on hiring youth, education, work	Sebokoane's herder
10 secs	filming context film crew evident	setting up camera for group interview
54 secs	herders lack of education, young herders prefer herding	Mashaile questions young herder

60 secs	complaint about boys lack of education link for text on problems of wage work versus herding	Thaole on boys not attending school
1.35 min	lack of work as reason for herding	Lebosa on work history, Mashaile on lack of jobs
2 min	lifestyle context	different activities of herders
2.03 min	life style context	Mashaile in hut, cooking
42 secs	history of posts	In Mashaile's hut, old man
4.19 min	history of posts & vegetation link to debate on grazing problems	Thaole on posts and veg

(NB can cut some of Thaole to just vegetation -reduce by 1 min)

50 secs	grazing problems disagreement with utility of govt intervention	Lebosa on hopelessness of situation
17 secs	filming context link for grazing debate	herders in Jareteng watching film
8.22 min	grazing, livestock numbers debate	Jareteng group interview
1.49 min	wool marketing problems	Jareteng group interview
53 secs	shearing & marketing	wool shed scenes and interview
20 secs	filming/research context	us riding
2 min	loneliness of the herder	Mashaile on winter conditions

39 and a half minutes elapsed time

Appendix 8

Script For *Balisana - Herders Of Lesotho*

00.00 no picture, text which outlines how the movie was made over what time span etc.
Steve and Chuck checking connections, image of herders sitting
Steve: its working now
Chuck: it looks a bit wonky
Steve:so we are rolling this interview.
Tim voice: what are you going to cover?
Steve (to Remaketse): Start talking to them, what they do as a herder, that kind of thing get into it slowly.

R.: what is your name?
-I am Lebese Tsita
-where do you come from, -from over the river,
-Are you herding
-Yes.
-your family's stock?
-my own and my family's.

Fade out to mountain scene
-horse rider going down Langa valley, (sekhaunkola music)
boy next to herder on horse,
Herder and sheep in long grass - Title: Balisana-Herders of Lesotho
herder feeding sheep with bowl
herders next to Mashaile's post.(colourful blankets)

2.14 min   Mashaile leaning on kraal wall (LB5)
I am Mashaile Kapa from Moseli Ntsiking. I grew up herding horses and I went to school up to standard 6. I had to leave school because my father had no work. I said to my father, no, I am going to work.
INSERT: Mashaile driving sheep into kraal.
I got hired by his uncle herding cattle at home. I stayed with my uncle for about 11 years and then I went to initiation school. After that, I herded at Thabang for Khaole. I worked a year there. He paid me with a cow and then I was hired by Thabo Tsita at Thabang. This is my fifth year working for Thabo. I now have 37 livestock. In the future I want to marry, having my own home. I'm still young, 23 years old.

I hope he has helped me in my work by the time I marry because here I am in a wilderness, I do not have the company of a woman. Here it is cold. It's desolate where Christ was born.

Pan of Tryhoek village to Noah and R.
subtitle: Tryhoek village, Noah Nkuni, stock owner.
Noah Nkuni, Loi's employer, full body shot, incl R (March 91 - LB9)
-R Is it easy or hard to find herders?
-It is hard, it is hard.
-Can you find experienced herders or new ones?
-These two herders satisfy me like Loi.

43 secs: Noah Nkuni, full shot to medium, in village (LB9)
-R. Do you pay him in sheep or money?
-I pay him in sheep.
-R. How many.
-I started by paying 4 up to 6 sheep, now I am going to pay him 12.
-R. Is it good to pay someone of his age 12 sheep.
-According to Basotho custom I find it good. Everyone of that age is being paid 12 sheep.

Loi herding by kraal:
subtitle: Loi Motutubali, one of Mr Nkuni's herders.

cut to Loi, group interview, medium shot (LB3)

-they say I am young and so should earn six sheep a year. But Mr Nkuni can send me anywhere, even if it is cold, and while his children stay at home, he pays me six sheep. This annoys me.

50 secs

Sebokaone's herder - in hut (March '91 - LB5)
- I like to herd sheep because I saw people who herded before me were gaining and I thought it was a waste of time to be schooling because I would not get animals to get married with (bohali).

10 secs setting up camera for group interview- March 91
33 secs
Mashaile, group interview, close up March '91 - LB1)
We don't know what the younger boys think of school, they won't say if their fathers made them come here. (Repeats himself).

24 secs
-(Mashaile) Why did you come here?
-(young boy with cap) I was herding, I did not like school.
-(other young boy) I was at school but we had no-one to herd at the post.
-(Mashaile) So your parents took you out of school?
-Yes.
-Did you feel angry about it?
-No.

116

1 min

Thaole,(blue hat) in group interview (March '91 - LB1)

> -Herding here is no good for young boys. They should be learning a job at school, like knitting and saddle repairs.They are here there are few herders. Ideally, men should herd. It's a mistake for the young boys to herd. They should get an education first. They should come here herding when they are old, like me.

Tape1,hi8,march92: Mareka by hut

> I am Mareka Tsita, one of Noah Nkuni's herders. I came up in December but will go home in May for the winter. Loi will then come for the winter and I will be back next summer.

INSERT: mareka leading sheep to kraal, just before section of

Mareka leading sheep to kraal, swearing (Tape1,Hi8,March 92,1.23.27.):

"What's wrong with them?, I&m taking them to the kraal, not to the land."

(1.26.32.)

-Stop it. What's going on, they must not make me angry; your mother's !*!, you are making me angry.

Mareka in kraal, chasing sheep,

INSERT Mareka's voice: (Tape1, 8mm, March 92(18.29)

> Mareka: when we get up in the morning we check the sheep first. Then we make a fire. Then we draw water from the spring. Then we milk the sheep and store it in the hut. Then we drive the sheep onto the land. We return and cook papa (maize porridge)and also give some to the dogs. Then we may go and fetch firewood. Or we go and find the big stock, if the owner comes. Otherwise, we visit other herders because I get lonely here. INSERT: visual of interview.

INSERT: Mareka counting sheep

> In the evening I collect the sheep and count them. If, like last night, some are missing, I go looking. Last night one was missing. I went searching along the ridges but I was not hopeful. This sheep was about to give birth. It would not come back even when called.

> While asleep that night, I heard a jackal cry. I woke up, took my blanket, stick, my dogs and my whistle. I went singing this song. I passed Mokhaba's and Mokhotso's posts to a dangerous area. I was frightened but I kept on singing, then it began to rain. I ran to Mare's post. He was playing a lesiba but I did not hear; I was thinking of the sheep.

INSERT: valley scenes,

CUT to: marabaraba game Tape 1Hi8, March 92, 43.02)

FADE TO: longshot herders by rock, young boy wanting to stick fight
(tape1,8mm,march92)
fade to: stick fighting 9tape4LBbeginning)
cut to herder spinning wool hiband dub tape)
cut to : herder fishing (tape2,hi8,march9229.14.)

Fade to fire and pot in mashaile's post (hi band dump tape)

22 secs
Old man and M. stirring pot
-(old man), why don't you make a tripod?
-I don't know, truly, but you see up here at the posts we cannot find wire easily.
-There is a lot of wire down at the dip.

22 secs
M. turning papa in pot with stick

48 secs
M. on what he eats
-Each day I eat papa and milk
-Sheep or cows milk?
-Cows milk, in winter I eat only papa
-In winter I eat only papa, ntate Alotsi
-T. and fish?
-papa only..yes there are fish here, and eland meat
-Eland meat? where do you get it?
-by the cliffs
-where?
-by the cliffs

30 secs approx
old man sitting, M.'s voice then pan to M and back to old man (Hi8, 3)

-which posts were here when you were young?
-what?
-cattleposts, how many were there in Langalabalele and Jareteng valleys?
-This was Ramorebeli's the top one was Tlaka's
-are you talking of Mokhotso's post?
-No Sello went there from here
Noah Nkuni's post was Monokoase's

CUT: Thaole, standing alone half body shot (March '91,LB4)
(cutaways to valley scenery and vegetation)
..... Now the land has changed because it has not got the same grass as we had
in the past. It is few and there is no Letsiri. Firewood bushes have covered the

whole land over there. There is much wealth and people are many. It is necessary that we join the improvement groups right away to get advice from the chiefs and Agric people to bring us peace.

17 secs
Herders in Jareteng watching demo film by tent, back view
shot from front, herders watching (music from concertina)

2.27 min
Jareteng group interview, Ntsikoane (old man knitting, shot broadens out to whole group.

voice (Hdr on right) we don't have any comment.
-(Hdr left) we don't have any comment?
-Yes.
-Is it because you understood what was being said.
-Yes.

CUT: - (Chere) I agree with what people said that the animals must graze on grazing land in a good way, truly.
-(Hdr left) Yes but did you hear that they can graze but we should be aware of the quality of grazing and whether the number of posts should be increased. So what can you say on that point.
-(Chere) the number of post will increase
-(Hdr left) It will increase?
-Yes
-even being aware of quality of grazing
-Yes.. it will satisfy the animals
-(Chere) the animals, because Basotho nation is growing so they will increase and the number of posts will increase
-(hdr right) Where will they graze?
-(Chere) they will graze, in this matter Basotho must limit their animals
-interjections-
-(hdr right?) they should be limited to how many?
- to 200.

34 secs
change shot, Chere talking with hand in front of mouth

-(Chere) because we see the land is diminishing (qepha -there is a shortage of land) but people are increasing, 200 is enough for the land. 200 is enough even if the people are many when he reaches 200 he must see what he must do. The land will still be sufficient.
-(hdr right) so we who want 300 will become dissatisfied
-(Chere) Hache, but you will be dissatisfied by mistake because you still see how the land is
-(hdr left) it is a fight for the land (to improve)
-(Chere, Yes its a fight for the land, for how they must graze.

-(hdr right) Yes, I understand how much land is available for the herds. But if I want 300 will we be dissatisfied.

-(black cap) excuse me, you understand if you are given this limit, we are not looking at one's life, we are looking at everyone's life generally....

-(hdr right) Yes

-(black cap) ...for everyone.

(cut)-(Chere) Mr Lifomo, I will ask you again. Can you see that when you get more and more stock wealth can you see that you will end up having things that fall in the rivers, not knowing what their use is?.. (interjection by Lifomo(hdr right)... We must agree here. Do you see what is being fought for is the land. It is diminishing. It is diminishing .. (interjections)... If you walk over there to that ridge you will see that the land is diminishing because there are many posts.

1 min
change shot to Ntsikoane (old man, knitting)

-(hdr left) Mr Ntsikoane?

-(Ntsikoane) Me? I was looking at my work. Ntate, the argument that I see i think everyone is looking at his own family. No one can say he is not looking at his family. According to the government policy, the land is not the same as in the past, there is a shortage of land. The breeding of stock is not the same as in the past, it is heavier now than in the past. In the past the land was in good condition/well.

Many people migrated from their places to Mokhotlong because of good grazing. But today our land is being overloaded (imeloa) by stock. Look now, in some parts it is being eroded. That is why it must be reserved for summer, it must be reserved for winter. This is the time for the animals to get good grazing in those places at the time.

1.49 min
group scene, Remaketse's voice then he comes into picture

-(black cap) You know last year I was at Mokhapoung. We the association (WGA) decided to strike because it is useless, there is no money.

-R. How did you decide to strike?

-because it was a long time since we had sheared our sheep and no money had come in and our households were dying. The money did not arrive...(interjection) we don't have to send our wool there...Ah, the officials work as if we are hired to them yet the animals are ours.

INSERT SHEARING SCENE -Carry on with voices of interview; mute sound from inside shed)

8 secs
pan from horses to shearing shed at Mokhotlong
20 secs approx
inside shed, pan across shed, shearers at work, stop on blue overall man shearing a goat
20 secs approx

man picks up mohair from floor, carries it over to grading table
5 secs approx
shearer puts sheared goat onto its feet, sends it running towards door

2.07 min
CUT TO; outside shed, R and mike in view plus interviewee
- For a long time we had good wool and mohair prices but since last year we received unusual cheques, the wool prices were very low. We asked many questions to the government about the low wool prices and the prices being low we did not receive our second payment for mohair, it being said that our mohair is at the border not yet bought. Its been said that the reason is the Gulf War. The second reason is the countries which bought much of the mohair like China are no longer using mohair. Even this year we are shearing but we do not know what the prices are and whether our wool will be bought. Maybe the government will try and help them to find a market for the wool but we don't know whether this will happen.

2 min approx
Mashaile next to wall (tape5LB,242)

Look at these mountains and plateaux, they are silent. Now I don't know about these people who go down to the villages at the beginning of May. It is only me who stays along with Sebokoane's herder who is up at the head of the valley, and Mokhotos's herder up by these cliffs. But all around here it is just me.

INSERT: view up Langalabalele, tape 1,8mm,march92 26.46
OR; view down from nkuni post, (tape 2,hi8,march 92:3.23, 4.54, 26.07)

(cut to tape 5,LB,350); carry on with voice on M.)
The harshness for a person staying here is such that sometimes when you get home people think that you are anti-social (khopo). But its not that because by the time people have gone down to the villages one has spent about a month not speaking to anybody. Now when you arrive there, people speak to you too much and you get tired. And you think all the people are staring at you but its not that but its because you have been away for a long time.

Mashaile by kraal (March '91,LB5)
INSERT: boy drinking from cup.

This wilderness wants a person who renounces himself (itela) someone who enjoys the sweetness of life will not stay here.

CREDITS sekhaunkola music (svhs)

1) Participant Herders and Stock Owners

Lebosa Jacob
Mokhotso Kao
Tumela Kao
Mashaile Kapa
Chere Lekhanya
Lekhotla Lekhooa
Rampeane Lekhooa
Lesimola
Matuoane Letjama
Koeneho Letlema
Letlema Letlema
Mr Lifomo
Manatanzima Maltene
Malefatsane Mape
Thaole Mofilikoane
Tsietse Mohapi
Mpiti Mokhachane
Mokhuta Mongtella
Lebabo Motsoane
Loi Motutubali
Khotsane Nape
Ntsikoane Nkone
Noah Nkuni
Polisa Nthontho
Phokatjo
Chaka Ramakoloi
Maliehe Rasupe
Saleoe
Puisetso Sepanyana
Shampane Shampane
Tsietse Tsehlane
Letseta Tsita
Mareka Tsita
Piti Tsoeu
Mokete Tsumane

2) The producers also thank the following for their assistance:

Tanki Alotsi - Resident, Mapholaneng
Mamosele Alotsi -Resident, Mapholaneng
Morena(chief) Thabo Matete - Mateanong village
Francis Ntlela - Ecologist, Range Management Division
Stephen Ramoleka - Resident, Ha Mekhoa
Mojakisane Tsitsa - Mokhotlong shearing shed supervisor
Chopo Motsekalle - Resident, Ha Nazareth
Ranstoeli Mekhoa - Resident, Try Hoek.
Mr Motsoabi - School Principal, Mateanong

3) CAMERA: Remaketse Letlema, Tim Quinlan, Steve Schmidt, Chuck Scott

SOUND: Steve Schmidt, Chuck Scott

INTERVIEWS: Remaketse Letlema, Tim Quinlan

TRANSLATION: Remaketse Letlema, Mosili Photlela, Tim Quinlan

SUB-TITLES: Tim Quinlan

EDITORS: Leon Duvenage, Tim Quinlan, Chuck Scott

PRODUCERS: Tim Quinlan, Steve Schmidt, Chuck Scott

4) Edited at the Audio Visual Media Centre, University of Durban Westville, Durban

5) A production of

The Institute for Social and Economic Research
University of Durban Westville
Durban
South Africa

1993